Seasons of Death and Life

Seasons of
Death and Life

A Wilderness Memoir

Maggie Ross

Drawings by Rosinda Holmes

**HarperSanFrancisco**
A Division of HarperCollins*Publishers*

Grateful acknowledgement is made for permission to reprint the following:

"October" from *The World of 10,000 Things* by Charles Wright. Copyright © 1990 by Charles Wright. Reprinted by permission of Farrar, Straus and Giroux, Inc. Originally published in *The New Yorker*.

"Autumn Firestorm" by Charles Wright. Copyright © 1986 by Charles Wright. Originally published in *The New Yorker*.

Excerpt from "A Journal of the Year of the Ox" from *Zone Journals* by Charles Wright. Copyright © 1988 by Charles Wright. Reprinted by permission of Farrar, Straus and Giroux, Inc.

Excerpts from the chapter "Raven" were originally published in *America*. Reprinted with permission of America Press, Inc. 106 West 56th Street, New York, NY 10019. Copyright © 1984. All Rights Reserved.

Excerpts from the *Book of Common Prayer* published by Seabury Press, 1979.

FIRST EDITION

Library of Congress Cataloging-in-Publication Data

Ross, Maggie.
   Seasons of death and life : a wilderness memoir / Maggie Ross—1st ed.
     p.   cm.
    ISBN 0–06–067024–X
    I. Title.
    PR6068.082S44   1990
    823'.914—dc20   89-46464
                                             CIP

90 91 92 93 94 HAD 10 9 8 7 6 5 4 3 2 1

This edition is printed on acid-free paper that meets the American National Standards Institute Z39.48 Standard.

For B
with love

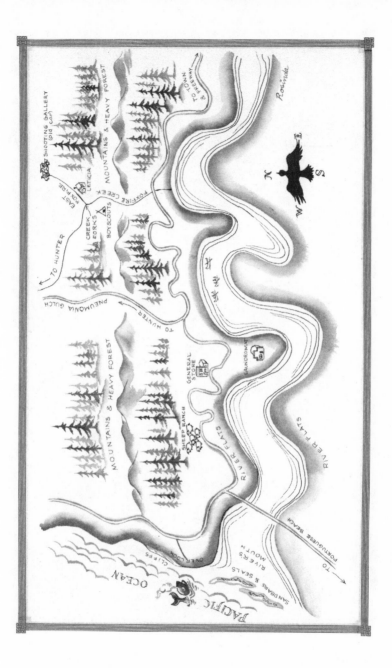

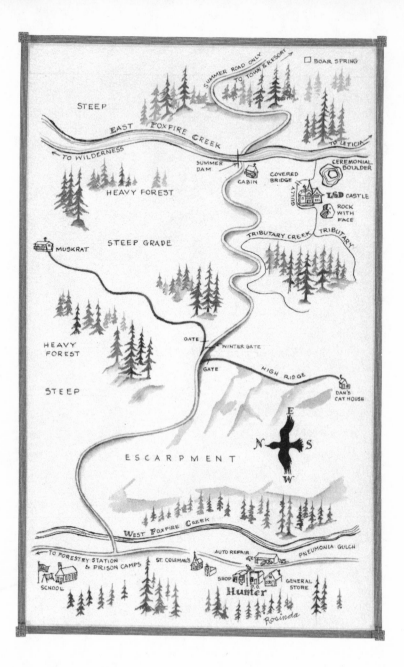

Contents

Seasons of Death and Life

The Abyss
of Dreams

Long ago, Hunter slipped from the mainstream of time into a quiet eddy. Its false-front buildings, scattered thinly along the narrow road that runs through the bottom of the fissure between the mountains, bask in the summer sun. It is soothed by the chuckle of Foxfire Creek tumbling down the fault, or startled from its dreaming under winter rains by the roaring torrent loosed from a primordial fastness.

Hunter is a real place, as are the animals and humans who populate this book, though I have changed their names and locations as I have Hunter's. Hunter is typical of many small hamlets tucked among the folds of America's northwest coast. Today you can still walk into any one of them and meet characters similar to those I knew when I lived close by in an isolated canyon.

All the same, I hesitate to say this book is nonfiction. Indeed, I begin to wonder if we rightly label any book nonfiction, because perception and memory, the filters of dying and living, pain and joy, hurting and healing, all conspire to make liars out of those rash enough to write about their experiences. "*I* don't remember it that way," says Muskrat, on reading some of these pages. But there were times when pain mercifully narrowed her perception to see only what she could bear, just as for me there are times when the process of healing colors memory as much as the throbbing ache of wounds that will remain open, however transformed, for the rest of my life.

Having said that, it is also true that memory distills: sometimes what we are permitted to recall reveals more truth than a simple listing of so-called facts, or efforts to be "objective." And it is on this unconscious discernment I have tended to rely, for the stories in this book are about love that is revealed in the most unexpected places.

They are particularly stories of the generosity and loving-kindness born of suffering that are so typical of Muskrat. In her self-distrust, she seems still to feel the need to justify these qualities, but in fact they are evidence of the nature of her being.

Her religious education came late in life, and the interior poverty of the fundamentalist sect only reinforced her sense of worthlessness. She has a hard time receiving anything she hasn't had a hand in. When I turn the tables on her, she looks at me with a fingers-caught-in-the-jam-jar expression, a wry, ill-concealed twitch of the lips mixed with awe and expectation.

But rarely do I have the last word. More often I am the straight woman and Muskrat the end woman. For if, in our particular minstrel show, she seems to get the worst of a verbal sally, she bides her time until she can hoist me on my own petard.

Muskrat entered my life when I came to live in Hunter. I came for its solitude. I am a hermit, or, to use a word less prone to romantic abstraction, a solitary.

As a five-year-old child I had an ineffable experience. From it came the gift of knowledge that, though life might seem free-fall through dark and light, indwelling Love, both the fire in the growing seed and the sun that attracts it, secures this free-fall, terrifying though it might be, as the only true reality, and the longing of every human heart.

As I grew up, I experimented with many traditional religious patterns. I soon discovered that too often form only has been preserved at the expense of content. Many "religious" people, as a result, are more interested in romantic projection and fulfillment of stereotypes than in learning the difficult self-forgetfulness of the exchange of Love with the Other. They use religion to make themselves feel good, and call it the search for God. They invest all their energy to create a fantasy world where they will not experience any pain.

This retreat from reality is perpetuated by the imposition of a counterfeit humility necessary to maintain a self-perpetuating bureaucracy, by which its members satisfy their desire for approval. Anyone who appears to threaten the "integrity" of this shadow world is immediately labeled enemy, dangerous, in need of control. These attitudes are compounded by sentimental, oppressive, always unhistorical, notions of what a "solitary" is.

Often during my pilgrimage to find a solitude where I would simply be left alone to live my life, it seemed as if I were a garden gnome that shocked and betrayed its self-certified owners by inexplicably walking and talking. I used to wonder if ornamental hermits of the eighteenth and nineteenth centuries felt exploited in this way, those people hired by the gentry to live in Gothic follies and be shown off to visitors.

As I entered the unknown waters of trying to live an old form of life authentically in the modern world, I lived next to one community after another, repeatedly encountering the same problems. Now I was going it alone.

I came to Hunter wounded, weary, weighed down by years of pressure to conform to external models. Though the "community"—the owners of the Hunter property—to which I was now responsible was more than a hundred miles distant, and though I attempted to find a compromise between the dehumanizing role of rhapsodic robot and an acceptable responsibility, inevitably I came to realize that an established order tends to interpret "responsibility" as unthinking subservience and material prosperity, and assumes that no one who is poor can be responsible.

When you're poor, it doesn't seem to matter what has been agreed. The employer controls the roof over your head and the money that puts food in your mouth. As Gustavo Gutiérrez points out, when you're poor, you don't count, particularly if you refuse to be cowed and exploited, and insist on the terms of the original contract. If you're poor, the very structures designed to protect you can be used not only to slam an impenetrable shutter on the truth, but also to disorient you, to make you question your own sense of reality.

It took years before I stopped being mesmerized by the classic doublethink of those who desire power (especially "religious" power) over others, who grasp this power by linking forgiveness with the fear of death—years before I realized that this technique is no more than the aesthetic fallacy that seeks to impose a destructive counterfeit of beauty at the expense of the Good, of life. And I was not helped in my search by my tendency to point out that the emperor has no clothes on.

In Hunter I learned that "solidarity with the poor" is a reality quite different from mere pious abstraction. I learned that those who preach such solidarity are often quickest to take the role of oppressor in the name of expediency. A lot of people in Hunter suffered oppression of one sort or another, usually from government or landlords, and sometimes fell sick from the associated physical and mental stress.

Before I came to Hunter, when one of my living arrangements would deteriorate to danger levels, anger would save me for a time. Often it seemed to be the only glue left holding my psyche together. Yet, even when the futility of continuing in a place became undeniable, it was never possible to leave at once. It took months to find a place to go; delay meant more damage, and a long period of recovery.

Ordinarily, we aren't alert to the effects of this sort of spiritual rape until it is too late. But on one occasion I received a warning: I felt a sea change surge through my body. Only in Hunter did the tide ebb far enough to reveal the ghastly creature that had begun to quicken in that moment.

Over the long haul, of course, anger is devouring. The time comes when it has to be let go, when wounds must be laid open ever more deeply to be healed. In Hunter I learned to live in the grace of the gift, to live within whatever time I was given, not to be subject to the fear that dictates physical stability at any price.

The silent gift was at work everywhere: in the happy chance that brought me to Hunter; in the beauty of the hills and forests; in the tapestry of light woven on the warp of giant trees; in water joyously cleansing the hillsides in spring; in Raven's practical jokes—the Eucharist of our lives celebrating every season through the years of terrible darkness as I waited to be healed and was being healed, though I didn't know it until I looked Death in the face.

The memory of my years in Hunter have the quality of an aboriginal dreamtime, though we were modern enough, God knows. A dreamtime—not a fantasy of unreality, but its opposite: a revelation of Reality that makes the times of our unawareness like a nightmare, and our awakening joy beyond speech. Part of this dream was the earth itself, a place held sacred, time out of mind, by the continent's original inhabitants. Another, the pain of insight that empties and vivifies the humdrum.

Of all the lifetimes within my lifetime, my sojourn in Hunter taught me the meaning of *sacrament,* through the smallest wood orchid and the vast wildness of the sea, through Muskrat's story, my story, every story. In Hunter the last flimsy boundaries between sacred and secular melted away. I was brought to adoration—often flat on my face— by continual encounters with the Holy in squalor.

Nonfiction or fiction? We forget sacred time in our preoccupation with the illusion of linear time. . . .

But even as I begin to abstract, I am brought back to earth by Muskrat's face, her eyes glinting mischievously behind her steel-rimmed glasses set in the slightly cockeyed halo of her silver hair.

I wonder what she is up to now.

All Hallows Eve, 1989

I

Settling In

Autumn Firestorm

The season steps up,
                    repeating its catechism inside the leaves.
The dogwoods spell out their beads,
Wind zithers a Kyrie eleison over the power lines:
Sunday, humped up in majesty,
                    the new trench for the gas main
Thrums like a healing scar
Across the street, rock and roll
Wah-wahs from off the roof next door to Sylvia's house
                    just down the block:

The days peel back, maples kick in their afterburners,
We harry our sins
                and expiations around the purgatorial strip
We're subject to, eyes sewn shut,
Rocks on our backs,
                escaping smoke or rising out of the flame,
Hoping the angel's sword
                    unsullied our ashed foreheads,
Hoping the way up is not the way down,
Autumn firestorm in the trees,
                autumn under our feet. . . .

                    —*Charles Wright*

Hunter

Hunter itself hasn't changed much since I lived there, but East Foxfire Canyon has been desecrated by logging and neglect. Muskrat still has her mobile home hidden on the ridge between the canyon and the village, where she is visited by wild turkeys, raccoons, placid does with fawns at heel, bobcats and their rowdy kittens. In the evening, sometimes, a stag will pause on the slope opposite, blue against the dark green hillside thick with live oak, bay, fir, manzanita, Oregon grape, madrone, and buckeye, a ghostly silhouette in the rosy afterglow of the sun descending beyond the far mountains and the river pouring endlessly into the sea.

Mountain lions still scream in the night; bears are returning from the north. Soprano coyotes still sing their weird antiphon with the siren that hunters set off to locate them as they wander the hills. The artificial howler is irresistible, but when the hunters arrive, the choir has vanished.

Steelhead and salmon spawn in the creeks. They run a gauntlet of seals and pelicans at the river's mouth, fisherfolk along its banks, gravel mining, and the perennial politicking over summer recreational dams. Osprey clutch twitching silver in their talons as they fly to nests they have occupied for generations. Mink and otter play among blackberry brambles, and secret their young in caves and roots of trees.

The ravens are still there, too. The tok-tok sound with which they signal among the firs, their gravelly croaking and bizarre mocking moans and shrieks rip through the canyon's silence and the white sound of its ever-running stream. And Raven's friend still steals duck eggs from Muskrat.

Over the ridge crouches Hunter, humming softly to itself, its bulbous middle, scrawny neck, and tail sprawled on either side of the road that meanders beside the main fork of Foxfire Creek. Its body is a cluster of buildings: a general store, auto repair, post office, and one false front occupied by an interminable succession of hopeful entrepreneurs. Two truncated spires look down their noses at each other from the ridgepoles of adjacent frame churches.

The earth rises abruptly on either side of the narrow defile. The west wall is covered with trees; the east is sheer rock, an escarpment exposed by the slowly moving earth— one of the countless, nameless fractures that wrinkle the coastal range, made restless by the force of colliding continental plates that grind against each other, twisting as they force it heavenward.

The ridges are softened by the pounding rains that fall between October and April in amounts often exceeding 150 inches. When the pressure of percolating water becomes too great, the hillsides burgeon and burst, avalanches of mud and trees slump into ravines, leaving jagged scars.

Redwoods growing up the west wall and along the creek mark the edge of the marine intrusion, which they crave more than groundwater or rain. They are the poor relations of gigantic forebears: a century of logging has left inferior second growth, trees rising from stumps. Some slopes have never recovered. New plantings are destroyed by mudslides, dirt bikers; by seasonal fires ignited by lightning, campers, arsonists.

Fear of fire smolders just behind Hunter's bucolic face. It begins to mount as soon as the hills dry out in early May, and reaches flash point in September. Until the August deer season has safely passed, and the first storm whirls out of the Gulf of Alaska to wash out the summer dams and saturate the countryside, emotional wires are screwed tight, and tempers snap without warning.

By contrast, in late spring you think you'll never dry out. The redwoods that line the road coming into Hunter create an atmosphere of perpetual damp—Pneumonia Gulch, Muskrat's husband, Eddie, used to call it. Fern grows waist high, moss inches thick, molds creep in every crack and cranny so that you long for the monotony of bright hot days to begin. Every hillside gushes, every gully is in spate. The water tank on the ridge across East Foxfire from the cabin can't hold the exuberant rush from the spring. Crystalline liquid sheets from under its conical lid, while the overflow pipe sends a stream of water three feet horizontally from its outlet near the ground.

People come to Hunter for reasons as various as the ways they make their living. Some commute to office jobs. Some ranch, or speculate in gold mines. There are jobs in the new mill at the west end of town; marijuana patches hopscotch across the rugged hills.

Beyond their often conflicting interests and life-styles, Hunter residents seem to share a common desire to keep some element of struggle in their lives in an age when struggle has become a dirty word. They may have generators for electricity, and new four-wheel-drive pickups, but there is a paradoxical edge to this materialism.

In country like this, you need constantly to be aware, to be vigilant, not just as a game—though there is always an undercurrent of play—but because your life depends on it. Everyone is alert for signs of fire or mud slides. People who live isolated in cabins scattered among the hills also have to be alert to vagrants passing through, or escapees from the nearby prison farm, and to the weather most of all.

If you want to stay warm, you have to know when to feed the wood stove, when to damp it down, open the draft, clean its stovepipe. You have to plan how much wood to cut for the next winter—it takes a year for the stuff to dry out. Cutting wood is not a leisurely Sunday afternoon pastime. Usually you have no choice of the conditions under which you work. Often there is no spring in Hunter: the weather shifts in a twinkling from dank to desert.

You drive your pickup as near to the wood yard as you can. You haul your gear from the back, your body already dripping in the morning heat. You fire up the noisy smoking chain saw, sweating with fear as it grinds through the tree perched on an angle of the hillside; you struggle against gravity to stay upright as you work.

You have to juggle the variables of steepness with the feel of the wood as the chain bites through, gauging the pressure you put on the handle behind the spinning, snarling, freshly sharpened teeth, listening to the pitch of the growling, laboring motor. You have to be aware of sparks falling into the leaf litter on the ground and the growing pile of sawdust, hoping they won't ignite.

You use gravity to make the tree fall—you hope—away from you, nervously tuned to the trunk's sway as you press the saw ever more delicately into the tree's eviscerated core. Fear grinds in the pit of your stomach with the pressure of the saw because you know you can be dragged suddenly forward if hidden rot gives way, or because the tree might begin to fall *on* you, and you must be ready to drop the saw, shift your weight, and run like hell as the tree crashes in an explosion of branches, twigs, dust.

When your body stops shaking and your eyes clear, you begin to cut the trunk into rounds, to roll and slide them to the pickup where you heave them in, or, if they're too heavy, split them by driving a wedge with a ten-pound sledgehammer. Your muscles tremble, screaming silently as you drag the long handle with its dead weight up through the muggy heat in one smooth motion to equipoise—then down, adjusting the angle of your wrists and the tightness of your grip to the force of the falling steel.

You are bone weary, but you are driven, because if you don't cut and split enough stove lengths you will be cold next winter, and dry firewood is expensive—if you can find it. Even the brash local woodcutters don't like coming over the roads to Hunter during the rains.

It was a late spring day about a year after I'd come to the cabin when Paul, the local real estate broker, passed by and saw me splitting wood by hand. He drove in through the open wire-and-pipe gate. I put down the sledge, wiped my forehead, rubbed my hands on my jeans, walked over to his battered blue four-wheel-drive pickup to pass the time of day.

"That work's too heavy for you, Sister," he remarked after we'd commented on the weather and the early heat.

I laughed. I'd heard that line when I farmed a vineyard some years back before I was able to formalize my solitude. Like my other critics, Paul was well over six feet tall and built like Paul Bunyan.

I gestured at the uninhabited wilderness around me: "Who's going to split it if I don't?"

Paul spluttered, then joined my laughter. His remark might have been chauvinistic, but it made him feel better when he saw my five-foot-four frame battle with that wood. It made me feel better that he noticed, but my muscles protested as I picked up the sledge once more, and I couldn't help a wry grin. I wouldn't have refused help. . . .

A few weeks later Paul came roaring through the gate again with a gas-powered log splitter in the back of his pickup. Before I could say hello he had eased it from the tailgate to the ground on a couple of boards, and was rolling it toward the pile of unsplit rounds. Here was a friend indeed, a helper helping, but not depriving me of my needful struggle.

But that was the second year.

The first woodpile I did alone and late, and I wore out before I got the job done. I burned the last of the dry wood while the rains were still falling. From then on, the dogs and I shivered in front of smoking, uncured logs in the chill

growers who, like the rednecks and settlers, sometimes shoot first and ask questions later.

It isn't safe to walk up the creeks in July and August. The first summer I was chasing trespassers off the property, one deputy sheriff told me that law enforcement officers started coming to Hunter only five years before. "This community did its own policing," he commented, and refused to elaborate.

A commune survivor owns the general store cum gas station. The store is stocked with flour, organically grown vegetables, pottery, kerosene lamps, denims, local jokes. A fifty-pound burlap sack labeled "Finest Sensimilla" flaunts the county's most profitable and illegal crop; T-shirts and ponchos with rain gauges silk-screened on them advertise statistics from the wettest years.

For sale are copies of locally written and printed poetry and fiction, and poetic in their own right are the notices tacked to the community bulletin board: broadsides for idealistic crusades, Amnesty International, a peace pilgrimage to Russia, the plight of the Navajo and the Hopi in conflict over rangeland in the Southwest; ads for Sufi dancing, day care, tarot reading, medicine wheels, women's consciousness-raising, various alternative therapies. There are lost-and-found notices, homes needed for kittens, and poignant, desperate pleas for housing: "Responsible woman with child seeks caretaking position. . . ."

Some of the older residents won't go into the general store unless UPS has dropped off a parcel. Then they stalk silently in and out with a curt nod to the long-skirted women who run the place, fill the shelves, take customers' money, trade gossip and advice with each other and the regulars, regard strangers and the rare tourist with suspicion.

The fourth group is the gay community, sadly depleted now by AIDS, who moved into Hunter's eastern borders from a nearby resort town and lived, quietly defiant, in isolated pairs scattered through the summer cabins. They also maintained a summer resort on the ridge across the creek from me.

They withstood harassment from the rednecks, ridicule, not to mention libelous attacks, in the local press (and sometimes physical attacks in the bars), and flourished. The survivors go to the larger town for shopping, mail, and entertainment, and keep pretty much to "theirselves," as Muskrat puts it.

As luck would have it, I met the manager of the resort. We established a working relationship, although I was supporting Leticia in her feud with its "furrin'" owner, who was encroaching on her land. Sometimes I looked the other way when resort guests frolicked in our stretch of creek, because during the most dangerous months of summer I would hear Tony's light pickup patrolling the road at midnight.

The familiar sound of his truck's engine straining down the steep grade across the creek would wake the dogs. In spite of my reassurance, they would become frantic as he drove over the summer dam and culvert, his lights shining through my windows. When I was sure who it was, I would breathe a prayer of thanksgiving.

I was a single woman, a solitary nun, and it was perilous country.

I Arrive

Before accepting the caretaker's job at Hunter, I went to see the property. It was a late February day so oppressive that it hardly seemed possible the sun still circled the heavens. Desperate as I was for a place to live, I was by now too cautious to take just anything that came along, but the psychological pressure I was under made decisions difficult.

I phoned an older friend, whose wisdom I trusted, to ask if she would go with me in her car. Rose is a tiny woman, but her meek, hunched frame contains endless reserves of courage and tenacity. A fine artist but a timorous driver, she was only too happy to scoot over and let me sit behind the wheel. We started west under sallow skies.

Rose first knew me as a farmer. We hadn't seen each other since I'd become a solitary, and she was shy of my transformation from winegrower to nun even though I was careful to wear familiar clothes from the old days. Her diffidence made conversation awkward. Once we had caught up on local gossip, the silences got longer and longer.

I had a sketch map and directions, and after an awkward hour we came to a sign, drunkenly askew, pointing off the main highway. On it was written the single word, "Hunter."

We drove what seemed like endless miles through Pneumonia Gulch. Beyond the buildings that clustered around the post office, we turned across the creek and began to climb steeply. Halfway up the escarpment, the paved road, marked "secondary" on the map, ended abruptly, becoming a rough dirt track whose surface was peppered with sharp stones that weathering had chipped from beneath the undercut cliff. It was barely wide enough for a car. The next curve leaned out into nothingness.

I looked at Rose. She looked at me with real fear. We both stared at the brooding wall.

"It says 'an unimproved road,'" she offered, reading the directions.

"Anything would be an improvement over this."

"We might try going a little farther."

But after bumping and jolting three hundred feet, we came to another curve so constricted, so littered with jagged rubble, that I stopped. Rose was white-faced under her gray hair.

"This can't be it. Let's go up that other road and ask."

I backed down the slope and angled up a steep dirt drive marked "Private." Fortunately, the Burns's fierce watchdogs were chained that day. Fortunately, too, Sandra was in the rambling split-level redwood house to tell us that the rocky track was indeed our road, and we should keep going. It wasn't the first time she'd given these instructions. The door banged angrily behind her as she disappeared into the house.

We crept back up the road, clinging to the side of the overhang. At one point the surface fell away almost under our tires. If we had strayed a few inches to the right, we would have crashed down the face of the scarp into the creek below. But once we made it past the drop, the road got a little better.

Abruptly, we came to a place where three tracks met. One forked up at an acute angle to our left, blocked by an aluminum farm gate. The second, straight ahead, following along the ridge top, was barred by an identical barrier. Between them, the way we followed plunged down the far side of the mountain into the darkness beneath the trees.

Where the road traversed the exposed face of the escarpment, the rock walls reflected what little light penetrated the heavy atmosphere. By contrast, the stretch before us tunneled through scrub, disappearing into deep forest. Spanish moss dripped gray-green from dead branches overhead; giant ferns stood melancholy guard over the boundaries. I switched on the headlights, but their beams were lost in the gloom.

It grew lighter where the road ended precipitously in a wide, fast-running stream that was swollen to the size of a small river. On the right, a ramshackle pipe-and-wire gate hung awry at the gap where its two halves met.

The caretaker was supposed to meet us.

I got out of the car and shouted.

My own voice came back to me, a dull, strangely muffled echo ricocheting off the canyon walls. The white sound of the creek lapped behind us. Nothing stirred.

The silence leaned on us. I shivered. Later I was to learn the weather of the place, its foreboding before storms.

The owners claimed to love and revere this land, but it was obvious that no one had cared for it for a long time. Plastic bags, scrap metal, bits of damp cardboard, old cans were strewn everywhere. I shouted again. Again, the dampened, sorrowing echo.

I turned to Rose. "I'm going in."

We had permission to be here, and I had not come this far to be defeated by some barbed wire and a few pieces of pipe—or my fear. Before Rose could protest, I slid on my back along the deep rut under the gate's twisted halves.

Just beyond, beneath the tall firs, was a streaked redwood cabin set on concrete piers. As I walked slowly toward the building, I stumbled over beer cans and slivers of wood. Paper and plastic bottles choked every grass clump, flattened themselves against the boles of trees, wedged into the grape-stake lattice of the cabin porch.

I climbed the rickety porch steps and looked out over some partially cleared ground toward the creek. Then I went over to the double French windows that covered two-thirds of the cabin wall to the right of the door. Green paint peeled from the sills. I peered through the dirty glass. Two smeared skylights were set in the steeply pitched roof, but beyond the outline of a ladder leaning against a loft, I could see nothing.

I turned to call Rose, shying when I found her right

behind me, wiping her hands nonchalantly on the seat of her pants. I should have known a gate wouldn't stop her, either.

"It's a neat cabin, have a look." I was falsely cheerful.

With a lot of work it *could* be a neat cabin. But right now it was a mess, if the outside was anything to go by. At least it seemed minimally weatherproof. Together we shielded our eyes as we strained to see through the speckled glass. After our eyes adjusted, we could just make out the white shape of a water heater squatting obscenely in a corner.

We left the cabin and walked deeper into the woods, down a gentle slope, watching the ground so we wouldn't trip over trash. Suddenly Rose grasped my arm and pointed.

On our right across a gully, looming through the shadows, was a house that looked as if it had been built by Hansel and Gretel's witch after she'd put a little too much LSD in her gingerbread. We gawked, unable to comprehend its bizarre architecture.

A turret had been stuck here, a hexagonal window there, a lopsided bell tower skewed all proportion, the whole huge higgledy-piggledy mass seemed poised to tip into the ravine behind it, where floodwater ate steadily at the bank. It was a unique example of the wood butcher's fantastic art. It was in desperate need of repair.

We crossed the gully by way of a short covered bridge on whose top perched the remains of a small room, and trudged up an incline to the house. Like the window frames at the cabin, the mullions of its French doors had once been painted green. They opened at a touch.

The living room went up two stories, like the great hall of a medieval hunting lodge. It was dominated by a wall of pointed windows on the left that reached from floor to ceiling, and on the right by an enormous stone fireplace set in the redwood. A hodgepodge of dilapidated furniture was scattered around the room as if someone were planning a rummage sale.

The beauty of the place shone through the squalor, and we could hear water singing down the rocks behind more French doors at the far end. But the whole place smelled of

damp; the floor sagged; mice and termites had left their dirt everywhere. Supposedly the parish occasionally used this house for retreats, but no one had been here for a long time. I half expected an owl to swoop down through the murk, brushing our heads with broad wings, hooting portents.

"Well . . ." I gulped.

"Well," said Rose.

We went outside the way we'd come in.

I burst into hot angry tears.

Rose, deeply worried that I had no place to live, quelled her own nervousness and tried to calm mine by saying, "Look, it's a dark day. You're tired and upset. At least it's solitary. You aren't going to find anything else like this. You can fix up the cabin. It's better than the tent you've been living in for the last two years, with the rain and sleet coming in. If it helps, you can simply think of this as a temporary home, and look for something else while you're here."

This was a long speech for Rose and it all came out in a rush.

The problem was not the dank and depressing canyon, or the run-down buildings, or the filth. The problem was me.

I had been looking for a place for months, but I wasn't in any mood to appreciate what I had found. In this ominous solitude, I not only would have to keep at bay the poison oak and blackberry that grew everywhere; I also would have to fight my way through an interior nightmare, the suppurating bloom that sprang from the series of human tragedies in my past.

At this moment, however, I was unable to see them as tragedies. My anger was decaying into bitterness, the bitterness becoming toxic. No matter where I ended up—if I ever found a place to rest—the price of my new solitude was going to be very high. A tidy chalet on a mountaintop might have salved my soul more than the depths of this abyss. . . .

I stopped crying and clenched my teeth.

"I've seen enough. Let's go."

Outside, the quiet pressed us down.

I was so preoccupied with self-pity that I didn't notice a peculiar set of charged messages in the air of the clearing, emanating strongly from an enormous boulder that rose thirty feet into the air between the castle and the creek. I didn't notice anything until the rapidly deteriorating light alarmed us by its color.

Although it was only late afternoon, we could barely see to retrace our steps to the gate. We scrambled under and got into the car. I backed it around and started up the hill. Our headlights glanced off the sentinel trees.

"Are you going to take it?" asked Rose, her voice hoarse and worried.

"Yes, I'm going to take it," I snapped, miserable at taking my bad mood out on my generous and loving friend. My anger began to crumble painfully at the edges. "What other choice do I have?"

I was already calculating how long it would take to walk over the mountain to the village to collect mail and buy supplies. I wondered how far the hundred dollars a month caretaker's stipend could be stretched, along with the meager income from my savings, how I would sell my weaving from this isolated spot. And though it seemed very solitary, I didn't like the signs of trespassers that were everywhere.

A raven winging over the spring green hills between the interstate and the Pacific Ocean would have seen a white van traveling at unconscionable speed, tailed by a sporty tan pickup. We'd been on the road for days. The van was loaded with a few begged and borrowed furnishings, a large loom and some yarn, Pierre, and myself. Sam, a childhood friend and carpenter, followed. He'd insisted I'd need him, and he was right.

I should have been filled with hope that bright April afternoon as Pierre and I tooled along, but I was numb. I was so numb, as I watched the exit signs flash past, that I couldn't remember exactly what the property looked like.

"Turn here."

We sped up the ramp, Pierre muttering under his breath, and headed west.

"Is it much farther?" he asked aloud.

Pierre had volunteered because he was curious, but he was also in a hurry. A small, brisk, silver-haired French Canadian in his fifties, he had offered to bring me to Hunter on his way somewhere else. Sam would stay for a few days to make repairs. After my first experience at the cabin, I mistrusted the glib and hearty assurances the rector had tossed over the telephone wires.

"About an hour."

We lapsed back into silence.

Mine was the numbness and dislocation born of a major life transition, the numbness of a released prisoner. Yet unwelcome memories of recent months stabbed through it like hot needles driven under fingernails, deep into the quick.

In my last situation, I had, as usual, believed the people who promised an environment that would nurture and preserve solitude. But I was wrong.

My insistence on solitude was tolerated, for a time, as an eccentricity. The others couldn't believe I was serious. They waited for me to surrender, to bow to peer pressure that intensified with each day. Censure replaced tolerance. What they did not comprehend was that I held out not from sheer pigheadedness, but from physiological and psychological need. For me, solitude is a prerequisite for survival.

Finally what had been simple harassment became overt efforts at disorientation. Black was called white; sickness, health; statements were made and denied; the relentless disparagement—vocation, personality, character, sexuality, morals, perceptions, theology, allegiance, humanity—nothing went unsmeared. The last straw, the only one that made me laugh, was the threat of damnation if I did not give in, relinquishing obedience to my bishop, my vows, my integrity, my mind.

In the end, because my bishop was far away, I consulted with a wise retired bishop whom I had known most of my life. Religion held no surprises for him; he was an expert in the psychology of groups.

We sat beside the sea and ate cheese sandwiches.

He listened to my tale: I was worried about letting the side down, about what people would think. By this time I was in the victim mentality bred by the rule of fear.

But I was waking up. I was beginning to realize that there was something here that had nothing to do with "obedience." It was something deformed and gnawing in the human heart: the need to control, the ultimate lust of making a person into an idea, or an object, for the sake of expediency. There were no limits to the means that would be applied to achieve the desired end.

"You have been given very unholy counsel," said my gentle friend. Then he told me a story.

A man in a Russian concentration camp was subjected to brainwashing. One of the most effective techniques in this form of torture is for the interrogator to ferret out incidents in your private, personal past that arouse unresolved guilt and undermine your sense of self. In the hours and days of questions, wearing the man down physically, mentally, spiritually, the interrogators dredged up these memories, jabbed them home, twisted.

But the man never broke. To each confrontation, he would quietly respond, "Yes, that's true. But I am forgiven."

There was a lot more, but these were the words I took back with me as I prepared to move.

Even so, I had terrible guilt. Self-doubt, self-distrust, and a certain courtesy that had been ground into me from early childhood, reinforced by years of monastic training, decreed that retaliation was taboo even in self-defense. This meant that my reaction to most frontal assaults, or demands to yield the secrets of my soul, was to blank out. At such times I would often have a sense of the earth moving under my feet. I simply couldn't believe people would deliberately lie.

When overwhelmed by verbal assault, I would feebly grasp at irrelevancies to parry the shafts that went home. Or, when the pressure became too great, I would be reduced to a torrent of emotion that made my most accurate insight inarticulate and diffuse. I despised myself equally for my impotence, my anger, my self-pity.

Only after a destructive encounter did the distortions of truth come mockingly clear—along with means by which I could have defended myself. Hindsight deteriorated into frustrated interior recrimination. These were the years before "assertiveness" was acceptable for women.

I had always thought, in the mentality of the time, that any anger was wrong, and I sought to quash, dodge, fast it out of myself. Gradually it began to dawn on me that rage was the only glue my personality had left.

Untruth and distortion are necessary to maintain any hierarchy, to shore up the unholy hegemony that maintains appearances at all costs. When outsiders came, we were told what to say and what was to be hidden, on pain of . . . The threat was implicit.

Without true humility and self-restraint, it is all too easy for communities—any community—to slide into what today we call "codependent behavior" or "cults." In those days, we had no name and no recourse. The tradition supported the sickness.

But even as we loaded the van and drove from the place that had been my prison, I knew that I would have to turn and face my fury, to sort it out from bitterness and recrimination. The price of my healing would be a racking between anger, no matter how healthy, on the one hand, and, on the other, obedience to the Love to which I was bound and in which I wished to live.

What I did not know was that the pain of this transformation would be greater than any wounding I had ever received.

These were some of my thoughts as we drove into the afternoon sun toward Hunter. I began to think of the thousand things that lay ahead. There was, too, the niggling anxiety, after Rose's and my experience, whether all was indeed in readiness as the mellifluous voice had promised over the telephone—with one small glitch.

"Oh yes," the rector had coughed, "except that a tree fell on the water tank and splintered the lid. An animal got in and died. Fred went down and fixed it, but you'd better bring some water for drinking until he gets in touch with you about purifying it."

Fred had duly phoned, and we were bringing jugs of bleach along with gallons of drinking water in old plastic milk bottles.

I dismissed the water problem, replacing it with an image of a clean-swept cabin, luminous from sun falling through freshly washed skylights; deep tones glowing in the redwood walls; a jam jar of wild flowers on a butcher-block table. . . . He had sounded so *welcoming*. . . .

We made the turn, unwinding the miles through Pneumonia Gulch to Hunter. We stopped at the post office to check my box, continued past the community church, the Catholic church—

"Who is St. Coleman?"

"The patron saint of camping equipment."

I tried to control my face.

Pierre looked sideways and guffawed. We turned up the escarpment and began to climb. The daunting, unpaved road had been freshly graded, and soon we were hurtling down the other side into the canyon.

But this plunge into the abyss was very different. Every tree trunk and branch shone with a translucent aura. Sunlight poured through green-gold foliage. Every blade of grass was limned with fire.

Wildflowers in unfamiliar colors and shapes grew everywhere, wildflowers with names as beautiful as their forms: shooting stars, mission bells, baby blue eyes, trillium, and, when I knew where to look, wood orchid. A doe and fawn leapt lightly from the road to the stream gurgling beside it, and at the bottom of the hill, the east fork of Foxfire Creek greeted us, sparkling, laughing, rushing in great noisy mirth. A kingfisher clattered by, electric blue, and ravens somersaulted in the fragrant air exhaled by the trees.

I was entranced.

Finally Pierre gave me a nudge. "I haven't got all day."

I jumped out of the van and opened the gate. This time I had a key. Pierre wanted to see the cabin, so we stopped there before going to the shed to unload.

Pierre was quick up the steps, but I lingered, bewildered by the sunlight, the unexpected beauty. His contemptuous hiss deflated my reverie. I climbed up to see what was the matter.

The porch was buried with even more garbage than before, as if dumped in contemptuous welcome. The French windows had nine broken panes. A foul stench poured out the jagged holes. Three cats appeared, rubbing against our legs, mewling for food. It looked as if they had been locked inside, and desperate with hunger, had burst out through the glass.

There was enough light coming through the sooty skylights to see the floor of the cabin, where a shocking pink sofa smirked from wall to wall. It was mired in dingy white shag carpeting. The fat water heater leered from its corner.

Sam had followed us and squinted at the mess.

"All ready for you, eh?" he snorted. "Open it up to air. It'll be days before we can get in here to work."

I moved slowly toward the door. I was listening to the day's top tune on my subliminal CD. For weeks it had been a chorus from the *Messiah*:

He trusted in God that he would deliver him, let him deliver him if he delight in him.

The repeating lament was warning, mockery, desolation.

But now, on the stinking porch, the music shifted to measureless Gregorian chant:

O spare me a little that I may recover my strength, before I go hence and be no more seen.

Pierre was having none of it. He stomped down the steps, revved up the van, drove to the shed, and backed in.

Sam and I held our noses against rug and wood soaked with cat pee. We rushed inside, flung open all the windows and fled, retching. Outside we started to laugh. I couldn't stop.

Sam gave me a shake, "Take it easy." Under his wild thatch of brown hair he was steady and concerned.

Pierre yelled from the shed that he was in a hurry. We ran down to helped him unload, and after a quick look at the LSD castle, he roared off up the hill, spewing rocks from his tires. We took our gear into the big house, dropped it in front of the fireplace, separated to explore. I headed for the kitchen.

In answer to Sam's call, I went outside. He was around the back side of the house, standing motionless. There the feeder creek tumbled over large rocks. It took me a moment to see what he was looking at, but when I saw, I couldn't breathe. In the natural rock, with the sun's finger gilding a fern that crowned his beetling brow, gazed a huge smiling face, a cross between an Easter Island head and a Buddha.

"It is the god of the place," whispered Sam, and I began to realize why this hidden spot was holy to the vanished Native Americans who had used the great boulder between the house and the creek as the ritual gathering site for their semiannual hunts. On it we had seen the marks of their ancient fires, and as I stood in that elemental presence, I was filled with awe before the energy that tensioned the air around us.

When I came to myself, Sam had disappeared.

I wandered down to the creek past the boulder. The bank was scored from winter floods. As I came to the brink, a great blue heron rose on slowly flapping wings from the shallows where it had been stalking. Auburn-crested merganser ducks splashed noisily down the middle of the stream, squawking.

I sat with my arms around my knees, caught in the gyre of sound and movement, the green–clear water swirling and sucking along the wooded fault, coiling around large stones, spreading into wider, quieter pools.

Sunlight flashed off the water. Pain pierced my mind.

I put my head down and heaved with dry sobs.

Muskrat

Sam stayed a week. His enthusiasm for being his own boss—and mine—enhanced his natural inventiveness, and generated enough energy to galvanize me from my zombie stupor. He would be up at first light while I lay snoring in my mummy bag, and had several hours of work behind him when he came in to breakfast.

Then he'd hand me a list of things he needed. I would climb in his pickup and head for the city, about two hours' drive from Hunter. When I returned, there would be decisions to make, and often a second trip over the same route.

The morning after we arrived, we braved the cabin's stench and tore into the dismantling process.

"All ready for you, eh?" snarled Sam as we threw the monstrous pink couch out one set of French windows onto the bed of his pickup.

"All ready for you, eh?" he sneered as our claw hammers ripped up the odoriferous carpeting.

"All ready for you, eh?" was his refrain in various tones as we darted outside for fresh air, coughing and laughing. I took the reeking load to the dump and phoned the former caretakers to say that if the cats weren't picked up in twenty-four hours, I'd take them to the pound. They came in an hour.

With the prime polluters off our hands, we were able to make the cabin habitable in a couple of days—window glass replaced, floors scrubbed, cobwebs brushed from rafters. Sam installed a wood-burning stove, made a redwood sleeve to conceal the sides of the cooking stove, moved the troll of a water heater outside and installed it in an old cupboard. We washed the skylights, slipping and sliding on the tar-paper roof. As light was released into the room, the redwood walls pulsed with fiery golds, browns, and rusts.

We purified the water, tracing the pipe, which was suspended across the creek between two concrete abutments, as it burrowed up the opposite ridge to the tank. Water pressure was courtesy of gravity.

We got soaked crossing the creek. The current was stronger than we figured, and we were gasping from the cold as we scrambled up the opposite bank through decaying bay and live-oak leaves, each of us lugging a couple of gallons of bleach.

We found the tank with its new conical roof crafted from a lighter shade of redwood than the base. It was a beautiful lid, carefully joined. Sam admired it with professional envy. Fred was a fine carpenter. We clambered up the lopsided ladder, opened the trap, dumped in the bleach.

Back down on the ground, Sam demonstrated the ingenious water system. The person who had enclosed the spring made sure the animals, who had first rights, could still drink without contaminating it. The overflow pipe ran down the side of the tank to a point just above the ground so that even small creatures could reach it. There were always a few drops a minute, even in the worst drought. But that afternoon, water was shooting out in a fierce jet.

It was marked "Boar Spring" on the old maps for the wild pigs that still frequent these hills. You come on them often unawares, their curly black bristles and flat faces attesting to their Russian ancestors, imported by traders for sport. They are dangerous if you corner or startle them.

The spring was surrounded by heavy logs set in a U against the rock face from which it flowed. We pulled off protective tarps, and the boards that kept debris out of the box, or pool, which was carved from the same stone. As the last of the covers came away, we stared into the still, pure water welling from a fracture into the hewn basin. Cemented into its lip was the pipe that ran to the tank, its opening covered by a small-mesh screen.

Sam reached in and gently removed a few leaves that had strayed under the wrappings. He showed me how to clean the screen that kept the pipe from becoming blocked with organic material.

We hunkered down, enraptured by the eldritch light, as if waiting for the spirit of the water to show herself, or faint voices to speak oracles from the earth's heart.

The spring's output dwindled in summer and I had to make frequent trips up to the tank to check the water level. I tried to keep it full, not only in case of fire, but also to maintain the tank's integrity. The water swelled the staves, which if allowed to dry out and shrink would collapse. Most important was to make sure there was water coming through the overflow pipe for wild things.

Often through the seasons when I sat in idleness on the cabin porch, my mind wandered to the spring. Always, when I climbed the ridge road, my eyes strayed to the grove where it lay concealed. I loved it more than the stream roiling and seething below. Always I was tempted to take off the coverings and stare into its depth. On the rare occasions I yielded to this temptation, my head was drawn downward toward the still waters through which flowed secret currents that forced it outward into the pipe. Always my gaze was caught by fires flickering in the spring's heart, flames that ignited a response.

One deep calls to another in the noise of your cataracts; all your rapids and floods have gone over me.

The day before Sam was due to leave, everything seemed ready. We had put cheap rice matting on the cabin floor, and moved my big loom, and the few odds and ends of crockery and discarded furniture he'd managed to scrounge, from the shed.

It was utterly simple and very beautiful: the pale straw intensified the colors in the walls. It was home. Or soon would be.

I made one last trip in the pickup to fetch Pomo. I had to have a watchdog, and while she was only a small mixed-breed black and tan hound who would rather lick someone to death than bite, she had acute ears and a sharp bark. At least I wouldn't be taken by surprise. She was named after one of the local Native American tribes because when she had arrived as a puppy her small brown face looked out at me from her blanket like a papoose.

Kelly, a seventy-pound, similarly colored, long-haired God-knows-what, was with her at Bullard's, my former next-door neighbor. His ranch was a good hour's drive around the mountains.

The back roads traversed a time warp as they wound through unfamiliar forest, then unfolded in old familiar curves among the vineyards. After four or five miles, I turned off on Bullard's drive.

The vines were planted on a shelf, or bench, about a mile above the river. The land dropped toward the river in a series of these benches, descending in a broad sweep. Everywhere vines waved graceful arms festooned with dazzling green leaves. It was a sight that never failed to bestow a deep sense of well-being.

My mood was shattered when I entered Bullard's house.

He seemed glad to see me, but uneasy all the same. Pomo had just gone out: he couldn't find her. Kelly was overjoyed, but cowered behind a large chair.

A knot began to grow in my stomach.

Bullard gave Kelly permission to greet me; I comforted him as best I could.

The awkward, shaggy, wolfish young stray had turned up at my ranch with a rope tied tightly, too tightly, around his neck. It looked as if he had chewed it and run away from home. He cringed at the slightest sternness in my voice. He was horribly gun-shy. Weeks passed before he began to gain confidence, and it was months before he was reliably obedient.

But I wasn't about to challenge Bullard until I had Pomo safely in hand. I followed him out through sliding glass doors at the back of the house to the terrace that overlooked the vineyards. I gave the piercing two-note signal Pomo had not heard for years. Behind us, Kelly started barking.

"She's probably 'way down there huntin' mice an' voles," said Bullard, nervously washing his hands in air. "You remember how she likes to dig."

Pomo was as addicted to excavating gopher holes as Kelly was monomaniacal about chasing sticks. If she were clear down at the river, it would take awhile for her to come back even if she heard me. I called again, and again.

Just as I was turning back into the house to wait, Bullard grabbed my arm and pointed. "Look!"

Far down by the river, I could barely make out a black speck racing up the vineyard road. She was running flat out, her legs a blur even with her old hip injury. The false joint, which replaced one lost in an accident, worked well enough unless she overdid it. Today she was definitely overdoing it.

And before memory had run its course, I was engulfed by hysterical delight as she dashed in and out in a mad circle, not believing her nose and eyes.

Kelly slunk out of sight.

I faced Bullard, demanding to know what was going on. After hemming and hawing, he allowed as how he'd lost his temper and beaten Kelly for no reason.

That was all I needed to hear. With Bullard screaming behind me, I opened the door of the pickup. The dogs scrambled in. They didn't need telling.

Late that afternoon, Sam decided to leave. He wanted to sample the rustic delights of the nearby town. I could hardly blame him; he certainly deserved a holiday.

But he was concerned: "You want solitude; boy, you're really going to have it."

I tried to look nonchalant. "I know . . ."

It was beginning to sink in how utterly solitary I was going to be. Walking would be good for me, I told myself firmly. . . .

Sam was in a hurry. Both of us hated good-byes. After an embarrassed hug, he jumped in his truck and sped up the dirt road.

The dogs and I went back to the porch. I fed them, and collapsed into a chair. The exhaustion of a lifetime seemed to hit me all at once.

My eyes strayed over the clearing toward the creek. I began to think about digging a garden. It would be marginal, because there was barely enough sun time . . . a few vegetables and flowers, possibly not enough for roses, and . . .

I jerked upright at the faint sound of someone walking on the covered bridge. I peered into the twilight shadows. The exhausted dogs were too deep in their slumbers to hear and, for some reason, I had forgotten them.

I slipped down off the porch. I hadn't taken ten steps when I was stopped by three deer standing motionless in front of me, unafraid, gazing mildly at my shock. Our eyes locked. I heard myself speaking to them in my mind:

This is your forest. I beg your goodwill, mercy, and tolerance of my presence here. I wish only to live in peace with you. I do not kill, and will not allow hunters in this holy place. I hope to have a garden and beg your self-restraint so that I will have enough to eat. May the glory and blessing that shines through your beauty always protect us in this solitude.

In their place floated the memory of another, similar blessing, received and returned. Five years earlier in a forest, but a few miles east as the raven flies, I had searched for a site for my first "official" solitude.

I'd scoured the hills, but could not find a place that was hidden enough, or had the right feel about it. As I trudged back toward the retreat house, something made me climb a small, steep, wooded slope. Surrounded by trees at the top was a clearing, a near-perfect circle. I knew it was right, knew I'd been led, threw myself face down on the ground to give thanks, to rest, to get a sense of the earth.

Rosinda

After uncounted time, I felt hairs rise on the back of my neck. I lifted my head from my arms and there, not eighteen inches from my astonished eyes, was a broad, wet nose.

The stag drew slowly back. We looked at each other for timeless moments until he stalked away, his great rack held aloft.

The image dissolved. I found myself staring into empty space, filled with a renewed sense of covenant and promise.

As long as I remained in the canyon, the deer never touched the unfenced garden between my cabin and the creek, or the hanging baskets and half-barrels cascading with flowers on the deck of the unoccupied castle, which was out of sight across the small ravine. At dusk I could see them feeding close by, and at dawn their tracks marked the ground in front of the cabin where they'd passed back and forth during the night. My roses grew there, below the rickety porch, but they never took so much as the tip of a bud.

I don't remember the next few days, or how long it was before the first visitor came. The delight of spring and the magic of the canyon filtered through a painful haze. My mind had come to a complete stop.

I was dully aware that leaves unfolded, that the mergansers hatched their young. But I hardly moved from the cabin except to pick miners' lettuce, which was young and tender.

It was on a foray to find salad that the acrid mental fog began to recede. The dogs were rambling nearby as I searched along the edge of the creek. They were still too uneasy to wander off.

They nosed merrily in the brush, tails waving. Pomo pounced, catlike, on a gopher hole; she began to dig furiously. Kelly rushed over, not wanting to be left out, and the dirt began to fly from his enormous feet.

Pomo paused for breath, looking around at me with her head cocked on one side, while her not-too-bright companion continued to dig, his front legs like pistons. She had a dog's laugh on her face; bits of leaf mold clung to her muzzle.

It was time for my part of the game. I asked wonderingly, with intense excitement, "Did you get the gopher?"

At this signal she yiped and pounced again, digging twice as fast as Kelly. When I moved away, they left their excavating until Pomo found the next mound.

Little by little, the mists that made it difficult to breathe or move or live began to lift. Delicate green fiddlehead, a perfect yellow lily, the still heron in the creek, shy river otters at play—each was a revelation. Steelhead and salmon were spawning, their silver tails flashing and shimmering as they dug nests in the gravel of the shallows, swimming slowly around each other in the stately dance of life.

Darkness and lassitude were pushed into the background by beauty, by the healing of strangeness, by the elements themselves. As I pottered along the creek one morning, I discovered an especially secluded place surrounded by trees and brush. A small waterfall tumbled into a clear icy pool, deep enough to swim in if I cared to disturb the fish resting among the submerged ledges.

In this bower I removed my denim shirt, skirt, and underthings. Using the clothes for a blanket, I lay back under the healing sun. The dogs rested beside me, Kelly snoring, Pomo rock still, head up, ears alert, guarding, receiving the minute sounds of the dappled forest, a sphinxlike expression on her brown, black-tipped face. Even when the sun became too hot, or the wind cold, or insects aggressive, languor overcame my reluctance to dress and go home.

Days passed, weeks, maybe. Time was suspended. I was unable to keep any sort of timetable, much less rise for Vigils in the small hours.

Songbirds would wake me, or ravens signaling among the trees, or Pomo wanting to go out, or first light coming through the window of the loft where I slept. I would get up and stagger down the ladder, fumbling coffeepot and water, renewing the fire in the wood stove. Shivering, a steaming mug cradled in both hands, I would go out on the stoop to greet the morning, to breathe the freshness of late spring. After I said the Daily Office, and sat for an hour in still-prayer, the forest would claim me.

Then one day, Pomo began barking in a sharp staccato stream, nose pointed in the air. Kelly joined her, snarling and snapping in his part-coyote fashion. I heard the engine shortly before a big orange four-wheel-drive county maintenance truck drove through the open gate. I locked the dogs on the porch and went over.

A man got out, shut the cab door, and leaned back against it, surveying me. He was medium sized, middle-aged, tanned from working outside. After all the time alone, it felt strange to be speaking to another human being.

"Can I help you?" I was cautious.

"You the new caretaker? I'm George."

He offered a hand.

"They're all wonderin' if you're still here and what you're like," George grinned. "I had to check the job the scraper did on the road, an' I thought I'd come an' see."

"Thanks," I replied, amused that I was already grist for the gossip mill. "Who are 'they'?"

"Oh," he laughed, "the folks in the village. You haven't picked up your mail, an' the postmistress was wonderin' if you're alive or dead. Around here, everyone knows everyone else's business, which is sometimes good, sometimes not so good. There'll be some who try you out."

Gratitude, laughter, anxiety swirled around me.

"Don't worry. You look like you can handle 'em," George tried to reassure me. "Just don't let 'em walk all over you, 'cause once they do you'll never have a moment's peace."

I thanked him for the advice, my defensive hackles anticipating the threat.

"Most of 'em are bluffers, but if you ever see a gang with knives, don't challenge 'em. You got a dog . . ."

I gestured at Pomo and Kelly standing on the porch, noses through the slats, wagging their tails.

"Good. Come summer you'll need 'em."

"What about the sheriff?"

"Oh, you'll find the deputies are pretty cooperative, but it takes 'em awhile to get over here."

At this joke on himself and the condition of the roads, he chuckled.

"Just be sure you take down license numbers. It might be an idea to phone 'em and let 'em know you're here. When we put the summer dam across your creek a few weeks from now, and the road opens through the woods to town, ask 'em to patrol it."

By now I had recovered enough to remember my manners, but George was still talking.

"Another thing. It's OK now, but come winter you'll have slides on the road, an' maybe trees down too big for a regular chain saw. Can you handle one?"

I nodded.

"If that happens, just give us a shout, an' we'll be over quick as we can. Now I gotta get goin'. Nice to meet you."

"How about a cup of coffee?"

"Not this time. I'll take a rain check."

George laughed again as he opened the door, waved, backed out, and took off, presumably to report that I was still alive and kicking.

The dogs had been concentrating so hard, and the sound of his truck was so loud, that we were slow to hear the faint hallooing from downstream. No time now to contemplate the implications of what I'd learned from George.

We went into action: the dogs barked with extra energy, as if to make up for being caught off guard. I gathered my breath and hallooed back.

In a few minutes a woman's figure appeared, crossing the covered bridge. I hushed the dogs and moved to meet her.

She walked deliberately, dressed in a tan checkered shirt and brown slacks, her face creased with laugh lines and furrows of sorrow.

"Howdy," she said in a firm voice, "I'm Leticia."

When she walked nearer, a sardonic gleam leaped out to meet me.

"Thought since you wuz livin' like me, a lone woman on this here crick, I'd come an' see you."

This time I remembered to offer coffee.

"Aw, I don't want to put you to no trouble."

This was country courtesy. She was very curious. Again I invited her.

"Wal, only if it ain't no trouble, but I shore would appreciate a chance to sit down an' take these here shoes off."

I looked down. Her slacks and shoes were soaked. "You *waded?*"

She puffed up a little as we walked toward the cabin. "O that ain't nuthin'," she demurred, pleased with my respect, "though it do sometimes get to my arthur-itis."

It was clear that it would take a lot more than arthur-itis to stop Leticia.

"Shore is nice havin' someone like you here for a change," she continued.

"What do you mean?"

"O them fellers that wuz here before. They grew mary-juana an' had all kinds of drugs, wild parties, an' trashy people 'round here. Caused the neighbors a bunch of trouble. Sold timber off'n the place, too."

"Did the owners know?"

"Wal, we tried to tell 'em, but they don't care. Don't seem right somehow to be such a cause of trouble to people. They're a church, ain't they?"

I winced. Where had I heard this story before? Was the property the geographical key to the local community? Was there any sense of responsibility in the parish? Where did this leave me in my obligations?

We reached the porch, and after introducing the dogs, I offered her a chair. "Now, how about some coffee?"

"Never touch the stuff, but I'd shore be obliged for a cup of tea."

In the next hour, Leticia initiated me into life in the canyon where she'd grown up, married, and continued to live after her husband died. She regaled me with history and folklore until my head whirled.

Animal habits: "Coyotes shore are gettin' bad. People let their dogs run, too—but I wouldn't shoot this one," scratching Pomo's ears, "she shore is a nice pup."

Neighbors good and bad: "Be careful of the Boy Scouts, they set fires every year. Nearly burned me out one time when I wouldn't let 'em on my property."

The parish: "State tried to run a road through here once to the wilderness area. I spent a whole day in court. Parish didn't help a bit. Don't even try to keep trespassers out. Gives us all a big legal problem. . . ."

But suddenly she grew shy, disappearing as mysterious-ly as she'd appeared, with an invitation to drop in on her anytime. "It's about a mile down the crick, just where the forks meet. White house on t'other side—there's only one."

Leticia became a close friend and ally. She'd drop up, or I'd drop down, sometimes driving her cows that she deliberately and illegally let loose in the summer to graze. Pomo acted as herd dog, barking with self-importance as she dodged kicks and chivvied the stragglers. Kelly was afraid of cows, and besides, someone had to guard the cabin. He'd bark the whole time we were gone, his voice faintly audible on the following breeze.

The visitors sparked my curiosity. The next day I decided to hike over the mountain to pick up mail, buy some fresh greens—the miners' lettuce was going to seed—and, whether I liked it or not, get to know the community within which I found myself in solitude.

I left Kelly on guard, which he hated, put a leash for Pomo in my backpack, and started off.

The three-quarters of a mile of red-brown ribbon that stretched uphill might as well have been ten. I stopped frequently. It wasn't that I was in bad shape physically. Two years of running up and down mountains where I'd last lived meant my body was hard. This was exhaustion of a different sort.

Each time I paused I was refreshed by the sound of the roadside creek, the moisture from fern and moss, and color: baby blue eyes, farewell-to-spring, Indian paintbrush, white-speckled trillium, green jack-in-the-pulpit, tiny pink petals the size of a pencil point clustered close to the earth—each in its microclimate of shady soft soil on one side of the road, or blazing sun and rock on the other. All around me the buckeyes, like chestnuts in full bloom, held their white candles aloft on the dark altar of the mountain. Their sparks lingered before summer's heat scorched them sere. . . .

The road continued on, winding around blind curves, diving into green and brown tunnels. Pomo scrambled up and down the banks on either side, her nose just off the ground, poking into clumps of fern and grass, and checking out tree trunks. Sometimes she'd slip into the stream below the road and stand hock deep, biting, lapping, dipping the water. Then she'd climb out and shake helpfully all over me.

This tributary also ran along a fault, and the land rose with increasing sharpness as we approached the top of the ridge. Finally I could see the crest where the road forked on either side.

For the first time Pomo trotted in front of me. As we broke into the open, a voice made us start.

"Don't let your dog run. She might get shot."

I looked up to my right and saw a short, stocky, gray-haired woman locking the aluminum gate behind a white Subaru.

"I won't. She's obedient. Come, Pomo."

But Pomo, oblivious to my embarrassment, sensed a friend and continued to sniff at the woman's ankles.

"*Come,* Pomo," I insisted. Finally she came. I snapped on the leash.

"I'd like to give you a ride," said the woman, looking me up and down, "but this isn't my car. It's borrowed. Mine's in the shop. Is what you're packin' heavy? I could take it down to the village for you an' leave it at the store."

I assured her it was not.

"See you soon, then."

And while I was still reflecting that she clearly knew who I was, while I hadn't a clue who she was, she got in the car and disappeared down the rocky track.

She was Muskrat, of course; so casual, our meeting.

I stood for a moment on the brink of the scarp, listening to sounds drifting up from the village below. Dogs barked, children shrieked, heavy equipment and eighteen-wheelers ground along the paved road, hauling logs south to the mill, or gravel north to a construction site. After the forest silence, the clamor made me tremble.

But I had no choice. I snapped on Pomo's leash, and we began to walk down the mountain.

At the bottom we fended off loose dogs, introduced ourselves to the postmistress, Carrie, and the ladies in the store, picked up mail, bought groceries, and escaped, footsore and plodding.

The road up the scarp on the Hunter side of the ridge was much steeper than the dirt track on my side. The sun beat on it, reflecting off slabs of heated rock.

By the time we reached the top I was sweat soaked and quaking. I moved gratefully under the cool trees. After what seemed an endless descent, we reached the cabin. I sat down on the stoop. Kelly, hurt that I didn't immediately let him out for attention, poked his nose through the slats and whined.

I reached up and touched his nose, but I was too tired to move. I was deeply ashamed of my weakness, yet there was nothing to do except start hiking again. I began to make resolutions . . .

. . . and woke up at dusk when, with restless hunger, Pomo poked her cold, wet nose in my ear, and when I jerked, started licking me until I begged her to stop. I fed them, said the Evening Office, went to bed, too tired for supper, too tired for still-prayer, or even to sit in front of the fire, as I loved to do, and wander. . . .

The next few days were quiet. I was able to recover a sense of healing, of silence, peace—until the trespasser blew it all to smithereens.

The dogs' barking was drowned by an engine screaming to hold a big black pickup on the grade. It stopped, blocking my closed gate. I was standing there when the black-bearded, slouch-hatted driver slammed the door.

"Please move your truck, and please don't trespass."

"Awright."

He spat over his shoulder in my direction and headed for the woods.

A familiar, awful sense of unreality came flooding over me, as if the earth were turning under my feet. Had I said what I said? Had he said what he'd said?

"I said," more firmly this time, "please move your truck, and please don't trespass."

The man turned on his heel, made a menacing gesture, and spewed a foul torrent, threatening arson, rape, and a good deal else I didn't hear, because something in me snapped.

I forgot I was alone. I forgot I'd left the dogs on the porch. I forgot I was a vulnerable woman. I went roaring out the gate and stood on the right-hand bank where the road went into the creek.

I was totally out of control—or maybe I was in control for the first time. I fired a focused stream of pent-up pain and fury at this boorish, law-breaking thug and his contempt for people and their property. Fueled by George's warning, I was out to make sure his experience of trespassing on my place was so unpleasant that he would never return.

As I continued to shriek, I was dimly aware and greatly frightened that I was unable to stop. All I remember is the red haze of rage. I don't remember what I said, or what else happened, but the man got back in his pickup, wrenched it around in a shower of gravel, and gunned up the hill.

I put my hands against a tree. It felt solid, rough, comforting. I stayed there a few minutes before I walked to the cabin to phone the sheriff.

As I dialed, I was anything but proud. I was appalled at what had been unleashed, at having come so close to cursing another human being.

I had no idea this power lived in me. I was terrified of it. I began to understand that the power was there because of so many years of still-prayer, but that if I were not careful, it would cause great evil.

A voice on the other end answered, "Sheriff's office."

I gave my report and the truck's license number. I must have sounded as shaken as I felt.

"Do you want us to come? We're kind of busy right now."

"He's gone. But could you please check out the threat? And come out when you're in the area so you know where I am?"

"Will do. Take it easy, and call us back if there's any more trouble."

As I hung up, I heard the dogs barking at the sound of an engine. . . .

Dear God, I can't handle another one. . . .

But it was a yellow Subaru this time. The gate was still open, and in drove Muskrat. She pulled up beside the cabin as if she knew exactly where to park.

I tried to pull myself together.

She looked at me straight from behind her spectacles, while Pomo and Kelly wagged around the bottom of her jeans, sniffing her running shoes, taking in the news.

"I would of come sooner, but got busy. Who was in that black outfit? He looked pretty upset."

"A trespasser."

"My God, what did you do to him?"

Don't you start, please, I can't bear it.

But she saw this was the wrong question, and climbed the steps to the porch ahead of me. I followed her, mumbling something about coffee.

"Can you handle a gun?" she asked, as I poured boiling water over the grounds.

"Yes, but I'd never have one."

"How come?"

I remembered the red haze.

"I'm afraid I'd lose my temper and kill someone." I tried to keep my voice level.

Muskrat absorbed this.

"But you're a nun."

"Yes, but I'm still human."

I poured the coffee.

Then she made a bewildering sideways tack. She seemed to assume I knew what she was talking about.

"I can cook 'possum real good, but it sure tastes awful."

"Huh?"

"It's really awful for a little kid to have to eat only what he can catch."

I finally caught on. She not only needed to talk; her talking would tell me a lot I needed to know. I gave what I hoped was the next line:

"It sure is. . . ."

And she was off . . . but just as abruptly jibed when her story began to touch deep emotions.

"County has no business closin' the road down here at the creek. Ought to be closed at the top of the ridge. Just because they put in the summer dam an' grade the road through the woods from Hunter to town durin' fire season don't mean people have a right botherin' us in winter when there's nothin' but private property down here. Ought to be a gate at the top of the ridge."

"That's what I was thinking."

She then unloaded a horror story about life on this side of Hunter under the last caretaker, worse than Leticia had told me. She painted a clear picture of the owner's neglect, its abrogation of responsibility to both the community, and to the property itself. Her tale confirmed my experience of the "promises, promises" attitude of the honey-voiced rector.

This piece of land held the key to the safety and well-being not only of my neighbors, who owned the rest of the woods, but also to the wildlife refuge upstream. Muskrat wasn't too certain about riparian law, but my time in the vineyard by the river had taught me a lot, and I had necessarily become deeply involved in county politics. At last I was able to contribute something to the conversation. As we talked, I began to suggest strategies to make our rural wheel squeak loudly enough to get greased.

Muskrat wasn't so sure.

"Tried some years ago to get a gate. They don't much care about what happens out here."

"They will." I could feel my heels digging in.

She sagged back in her rice-straw chair and gave me another penetrating look. "How do you know?"

"I've dealt with these county characters before. I'll write the first letter today. I can't go on with the sort of thing that happened just now."

"Yeah, an' it'll get worse come summer after the crossin' goes in an' the road goes clear through. Those sons of guns don't give a shit—excuse me—what they do."

She watched to see how I would react to this mild profanity, one of many that laced Hunter's dialect in the flow of ordinary speech.

"In the summer they go through here like bats from the hot place, light fires, an' tear up the landscape somethin' awful. They trespass an' shoot anythin' in sight, in or out of season. They used to have brawls down here."

"Sounds like I'll have to clean up the neighborhood."

"Yeah, you be careful. That bastard you run off was up to no good. That's why I come down."

"How did you know?"

"I knew."

Muskrat's telepathic abilities, I was to discover, were equaled only by the phenomenal education she'd given herself. That she spoke the local dialect concealed the fact that she'd passed the state nursing exam with a high school equivalency certificate and no formal training.

But brilliance ran in the family. During the war her mother, whose education stopped at the fourth grade, passed an exam that won her an electrician's job at the naval base in the next county.

At this point Muskrat shook off further talk and got to her feet. "You call if you get trouble, hear? I gotta go down to Rachel's."

Who is Rachel . . .

I thanked her. What might happen to a trespasser who ran into Muskrat was something I didn't care to contemplate. But I felt a lot better knowing she was on top of the ridge, even if it did take twenty minutes door to door. I followed her down the steps.

"Oh yeah," she said as she opened the back door of her car, "I nearly forgot." She handed me an apple pie, and before I could respond, slammed the doors, started the engine, and headed for Hunter.

The Leper at
the Laundromat

Within a month, life in the canyon took on aspects of ritual.

The alarm would go off at three, if I hadn't awakened earlier, and my eyes would open to moonlight and starlight seeping through tree shadows. I dared look out the loft window for a moment only, knowing I would fall back to sleep if I didn't get up. I'd climb down the ladder, light a fire, make coffee, pray the Office, sit in still-prayer.

Between six-thirty and seven, the phone would ring— or, if it hadn't, I'd dial. Muskrat worried about my safety; I was glad for her concern.

"You could at least let it ring," the person phoning would say when the receiver at the other end was picked up before the line buzzed (in Hunter, the timing of the ringing sound on the line had no relation to the phone ringing in the house).

"It did ring!" the other would say in mock outrage.

Or when I phoned her early because I was going into the woods, she'd answer, "Howdy," or "Good morning." This way of answering was typical of Hunter, not just of Muskrat.

Eddie, her husband, would have been up for hours, but sometimes Muskrat lingered in bed.

"What time is it?"

I'd tell her.

"Well, I guess I'm going to have to get up, since you won't turn off that big bright light out there."

Muskrat and Eddie slept on a screened porch; the morning sun fell upon the bed.

"Did you hear them coyotes last night? The dogs was barkin' somethin' awful."

We discussed the daily wildlife and weather report.

"What you gonna do today?"

This was a prelude to feeling out my mood. It meant she was hatching a plot, and wanted me as accessory. The next year, the spring after I arrived, we would talk about hauling mushroom compost and what we were going to plant in our gardens. Two years later, the summer after Eddie died, the conversation was most often about cutting wood. She had a big truck and bigger chain saw; I could handle the chain saw, she the truck.

"I haven't got that far," I'd say. "How 'bout you?"

While I was in the habit of letting the day unfold, our friendship was developing to the point that I began to fear for my solitude. Although the desert mothers and fathers did a lot of visiting back and forth—the law of hospitality was absolute—and went to town to sell their wares and buy supplies, I wondered where to draw the line. At the same time, I had no illusions about who was receiving charity.

"Lessee," Muskrat would sigh, "my brain isn't function-in' yet."

"So what else is new?"

"Oh hesh, that's not nice. How come you're always pickin' on me? I hadn't noticed yours was in the greatest workin' order."

After a moment's silence, she'd add, "Where's that nice cup of black coffee you were supposed to bring me?" Her tactics were taken from the French cavalry manual: *When in doubt, attack.*

"I'll bring it up to you, but it'll be cold by the time I get there. Do you want it in a cup or IV?"

"Well, I guess I'm going to have to get out of this bed."

"Why'd you want to do a thing like that?"

"Well, for one thing, I don't have a large jar here. How come you haven't invented the external catheter yet?"

"This conversation is deteriorating."

We'd laugh and go about our business, but chances were that sometime during the day, the dogs would announce the arrival of the yellow Subaru. It zipped down the road, slewed through the gate, stopped by the steps. I usually had hot coffee made. We'd sit and talk.

At first she questioned me about my life. I tried to explain that while solitude was primarily a way of the heart, I needed physical solitude, too, that a life dedicated to solitude emphasizes one aspect of every person's life, building as much on weakness as anything. To break through the mythology surrounding nuns, much less solitaries, was an uphill struggle.

I came to Hunter thinking I'd have total solitude. I was wrong. I had plenty, but I hadn't realized how much I needed what Muskrat provided, or what, evidently, I provided for her. There was a blessed mutuality that reflected, in its ordinariness and informality, the ancient desert tradition of manifestation of thoughts.

As we sat nursing our coffee mugs, she'd suddenly deliver herself of another *non sequitur:* "It's awful when little babies die." Or, "It's terrible when a mother beats a little kid so they won't cry." Or, "Nobody knows the pain of a little child what's been raped by an adult."

At first I didn't know whether to probe or not. But as time passed, I swallowed my hesitation. She'd tell things in fits and starts, and sometimes had to be helped, but she let me know when she wanted help. She seemed to feel that I knew much more than I did, and sometimes I stopped trying to understand the references in her narrative, and, as she called her thoughts with soft cries from the tangle of memory, simply let pictures form in my mind.

When it all got to be too much she'd say, "Well, I gotta get goin'," but before she got back into her car, there was invariably a gift of fruit or venison, vegetables from her garden, or a freshly baked pie.

She needed to mother, and I needed a mother.

She needed to talk, and I needed to be needed.

She needed to bleed, and my festering wounds needed opening by hers.

I was humbled by her trust. One day I asked how come she confided in me when she refused to let others get close.

"I dunno," she sighed. "It just seemed like that first day at the gate I always knew you."

She was mock impatient with my ignorance. "Gee," she would say, mischief crinkling her eyes and mouth, "don't you know nuthin'?" Or, "Didn't I tell you that? I was sure I told you."

The brutality, deprivation, and hardship she had endured would have destroyed women less resilient. Others might have used a similar history to justify inflicting vengeance on the world in exchange for the pain of life. She had rejected this option in the past, and continued to reject it.

She strained to overcome the natural desire to hurt those who had hurt her. She'd outline ways of getting her own back, but even as the words raised spectres obedient to her thoughts, she'd dismiss them, saying, "But that just don't set right somehow."

It wasn't priggishness—the struggle was real. It was rather a lifelong pattern that focused an instinct for truth, a decision held in the face of suffering I could hardly imagine.

Oh, she had her bitterness, her resentments, her unfor-givingness. I don't want to make her out to be a plaster saint. But she never ran from her broken life, and she delighted in all creatures as they wandered in and out of it, warts and all. She chose to face pain and to move within it to truth, to new life that at first hardly seemed life at all, and slowly became ordinary.

To support her children she became a nurse. She said she just happened on the job. "Jan wanted to go to the Adventist Academy, an' I didn't have the money. So I went an' took the test, even though I didn't have the education, an' I passed."

She had a surefire formula for doing multiple-choice—that was her excuse, anyway. She advanced quickly, training as a psychiatric nurse in a large state institution for the mentally and physically handicapped, one of those places society uses to shove out of sight reminders of a mortality it has neither the guts nor the compassion to embrace. She had a real gift for this kind of nursing, and her gift was recognized. She was sent to courses in teaching hospitals.

Nursing the severely handicapped is emotionally demanding work. She kept at it for nearly twenty years, carrying more and more responsibility. Her knowledge of medicine, her diagnostic skill and pharmacological insight, were staggering. This background explained some of her canniness about other people, less damaged in body and mind, but disabled in spirit.

I tried to penetrate the source of her simple love and understanding for the incompletely formed scraps of humanity for which she had cared. Her self-giving was in part her need to be needed, her way to make herself a place in the world that had so often rejected and abused her. But underneath was an almost incomprehensible generosity.

The wellspring of her love was the very suffering she had experienced. She drew on her deep, never-healed wounds to choose the way she would endure, and for the strength with which they were infused. Evidently she had first made this choice at a very early age.

"Religion" had nothing to do with it. In her maturity, she was, briefly, a Seventh-day Adventist. "I finally told them to take me off the rolls," she told me apologetically one morning. "Religion just didn't touch what I'd done and been, somehow; it seemed all about the outside, an' nuthin' about the inside. Besides, there was all that footwashin', and while I didn't mind doin' the washin', I couldn't stand bein' washed."

I couldn't stand to be washed.

After she left I just sat. Her tales lanced my wounds, still leeching acid through their rags, inflaming the rage that infected me; more, the hatred of the rage; the desire for vengeance; the desire to be free from the prison of these violent feelings. I wanted to be washed, but I was too frightened and proud; I wanted to be healed, but the prospect of health was terrifying.

As a result, the turmoil I tried to suppress with physical work or study would surface, and I would be thrown again between extremes that were somehow identical. On the one hand, the purifying fire, the Love to which I longed to be obedient, and, on the other, the parched watering place of tears that would not come, tears I needed for cleansing and relief, no matter how they burned.

Sometimes I tried to run away from this torment. I'd take the dogs and roam the forest; I'd chop wood; I'd weave. Weaving was often the worst thing I could do, because whatever I was experiencing was threaded with the yarn. I promised prayer and blessing with the weaving I sold, not rage and cursing. Whether I was pulling it through heddles, or throwing the shuttle, the pattern of my inner life was ineluctably exposed to me, even if I preferred not to see it.

It took years before I understood a letter I received around this time. The anguished struggle to forgive, wrote this spiritual parent, is itself the forgiveness. As long as I willingly endured it, I would be healed and so would the others, even though they did not know. This insight was too much like being washed, and I was not yet ready to trust again wholly, not even God.

The trespassers got the worst of my anger. As summer waxed hot, they became a plague. It was impossible to avoid them. I told myself—truly as it turned out—that if I were tough this first year, other summers would be easier. But I hated every confrontation, for each rehearsed and fed the very anger I wished to be rid of.

Toward summer's end, I was hassled to a hair trigger. What got to me was the trespassers' deliberate, overt lying, the disorienting tactic of saying "I'm not going to trespass" and proceeding to do exactly that, or, caught with smoking gun in hand, declaring with innocent outrage, "I wasn't shooting fish." At such moments the world seemed to spin under my feet, whirling me into the vortex of emotion.

I never would have survived without the dogs. I trained

them to bark on command. Kelly had a ferocious display, leaping at the end of his leash, almost yanking it from my hands, snapping his teeth with audible clicks. If I'd let him loose he would have turned and run, but the leash gave him courage.

I made friends with the deputies and with the game warden, who lived miles upstream in the wilderness area. With their help, I honed my performance so that the trespassers received maximum flak with minimum danger to me. The deputies were good about follow-up when I recognized the person, or memorized a license number. Gradually word got around that a harpy lurked in the canyon, and if you wanted your macho ego left intact, you'd better do your trespassing somewhere else.

I wasn't proud of this reputation. It was tremendously painful to confront trespassers, because everything to which I was dedicated bound me to reconciliation, to gentleness and healing. But it's one thing for a man to exhibit these virtues in a situation such as mine, and quite another for a lone woman. Too often men seem to take a woman alone as a challenge.

But defending property was hardly my vocation, no matter whose it was, or how much the law was on my side, or the fact that it was my job. It was the wrong job. It only added to my inner conflict. That my effectiveness came from acting out my rage was an irony I was forced to embrace.

Each time I lost my fragile control—sometimes deliberately, if the situation got really bad—I returned to the cabin and wept without tears. My body was a single silent cry begging for pity: pity for the poor trespasser, pity for the cup of bitterness I had to drink to the dregs, the only medicine that would heal me; pity that would prevent each new eruption from rooting fury in my very being.

I said, "I will keep watch upon my ways, so that I do not offend with my tongue.

I will put a muzzle on my mouth while the wicked are in my presence."

So I held my tongue and said nothing; I refrained from rash words, but my pain became unbearable.

My heart was hot within me; while I pondered, the fire burst into flame; I spoke out with my tongue:

Lord, let me know my end and the number of my days, so that I may know how short my life is.

We walk about like a shadow, and in vain we are in turmoil . . . And now, what is my hope? O Lord, my hope is in you.

Deliver me from all my transgressions and do not make me the taunt of the fool.

I fell silent and did not open my mouth, for surely it was you that did it.

Take your affliction from me; I am worn down by the blows of your hand. . . .

Gradually I began to understand that I could have no part in my own healing. I could only be willing to be healed, to allow the wounds, to acknowledge the terrible emotions and feelings, to wait, to let the fiery current run its natural course and burn itself out. Muskrat's stories were part of this healing process.

But there were other ironies, other paradoxes. Some threw me into fire; some threw me into water.

The rector came to visit, he of the mellifluous voice that promised everything and delivered very little. I had reported the appalling state of the property when I arrived, the tree rustling, the geographical key to the community, the legal ramifications of letting people through without protest.

"Do whatever you think right" was all the rector had ever said over the phone.

I doubted he would back me if I were challenged. I could tell he wasn't listening, and even if he were, that he didn't believe me.

A week after his visit, Fred came down to make some repairs and confirmed my impression. The rector had picked up a hitchhiker on the way home, who boasted that he'd helped cut and sell the trees.

"So you were right," the rector was to remark in a later call. But when confronted by vestry members, he denied believing a drifter's story in preference to mine—the drifter being a man, and I a woman. As luck would have it, a young vestryman was with him that day. Power had not yet so corrupted him that he would support the lie.

The plight of the land, the creatures, and the community was now my own. I suggested means by which the place could become self-supporting on a tiny budget, without violating the forest, or intruding on my solitude. The vestry was interested, but the rector's words on his visit this day, were belittling.

"Never underestimate little Sister Maggie," he cooed dreamily, tickled that a mindless little nun might really be capable of facts or figures, much less the truth of the matter.

"Such a beautiful canyon," he mused, standing with one hand on the porch rail, surveying the staked-out garden and the creek. "Just say your prayers and love your dogs."

Yes, sir. Sorry. I forgot I'm a garden gnome.

"By the way," he crooned, "there's a personal favor you could do me . . ."

Oh brother. Now what.

"I want you to be my spiritual director."

I fought to keep a straight face. "I'm afraid that's not possible."

Look out! The statuary walks and talks!

"What did you say?"

"I said, I'm afraid that's not possible."

"Why not?"

It's the old, universal story: you want me to confirm in you everything that is destructive to yourself and to others. You want me to reassure you that making yourself feel good is the same as the journey into God. You want to decorate your ego with an exotic.

"I have an absolute rule that I never agree to relationships that could be called 'spiritual direction.'"

"That's ridiculous. Certainly you can be my director."

And hallow your power trip? Not on your life. Or mine.

"I'm afraid not. You're welcome to come and talk any time you like. But the title 'spiritual director' is itself destructive, and besides, there are times when I don't answer the phone or letters, and won't see people. Someone in that role has to be available."

"That doesn't bother me."

But it bothers me. You want me to tell you what you want to hear and then shift responsibility by claiming, "My spiritual director said . . ." You want to keep me for a pet, while pretending obedience.

"Yes, but it bothers me. People usually ask for the wrong reason."

"Do you think I'm doing that?"

There's the first note of threat.

"That's not for me to say."

But it is for me to say, because without integrity, relationships that call themselves sacred become demonic. And I doubt you could bear what you would see, if one day you got serious.

"What's the wrong reason?"

"To be able to tell other people that you have a solitary for a spiritual director."

"Oh come on. You don't have to worry about that with me."

But I do.

"Please, I'd really rather not. There are a lot of other reasons . . ."

Let's see what he does when a woman says no.

The rector turned to look at me, leaned forward, and hissed, "If you're going to stay here, I think you had better be my spiritual director."

. . . O spare me a little that I may recover my strength, before I go hence and be no more seen. . . .

OK, Maggie, decision time. Are you woman or mouse?

Mouse.

Coward.

But I'm too exhausted to move on just yet. Besides, I should give him a chance. It's just possible that . . . and there's Muskrat.

Muskrat you have always with you. And then?
When then comes, I'll see.
"Well?" He hitched one leg up on the rail, amused. I was glad to be sitting down.
"On one condition."
"What's that?"
"That you don't tell anyone. The confidentiality, for your sake and mine, must be absolute."
"Sure, sure, no problem, you know that. Now where do you want to start?"
I know there's a problem, and I don't want to start.
"Do you know how to meditate?"
"No. I'm much better at making community."
How can you possibly make community without. . . .

Two days later Fred phoned to arrange the day for his repair trip.
"I hear you're now the rector's spiritual director."

The rector left me alone for six months. Then we had a conversation about finances.
". . . but of course I don't have to pay for my stay there or anyone I, as Rector, send down. That's my privilege."
"The money's got to come from somewhere if this place is to stay afloat. Otherwise you're asking an insolvent project to subsidize the richest parish in the diocese."
I thought your love for this canyon was genuine. Or is it only an executive perk?
"I can't stand strong-minded women," shouted the rector, slamming down the phone.
I managed to control myself by having a fantasy about testifying in a federal court, holding a press conference on discrimination against women. Maybe the rector picked up my thoughts, because half an hour later he phoned back.
"Soul friend," he whined.
"That's it," I cut him off. "I'm not your director any longer. It's not a relationship in which emotional and spiritual blackmail have any part."

As soon as I said it, I knew I'd signed my exit papers.

I put the receiver quietly down, extinguishing the ranting voice, and walked outside.

Autumn lay dying. A golden veil glittering with motes hung in the canyon. Even the plashing of the creek was muted as we waited for the rains. The birds stilled their twittering. I heard ravens call, soaring too high for me to see.

≈≈≈

But there was always Muskrat. With her, the most mundane tasks became an adventure. For instance, there was the time we went to do laundry.

Both of us hate to do laundry.

Our clothes were grimy from heat, heavy chores, dust, oil, less analyzable forms of grime. Neither of us had the water supply, much less electricity, to run a washer. So when Muskrat first proposed we do laundry together, I jumped at it.

I have several venal reasons for liking to do laundry with Muskrat, aside from clean clothes. In spite of my sometimes brash exterior, I'm shy. If Muskrat and I are engrossed in our gossip, people hesitate to break in.

In addition, between us, Muskrat and I can claim enough washers and driers to beat the competition. This selfishness helps get the job done as quickly and painlessly as possible. And Muskrat is my newspaper. There are other reasons, equally crass.

I relate all this just in case you have ideas about laundry as penance, or my charitable motives.

One hot June morning, Muskrat and I headed for the coin-op, timing our arrival, as usual, about ten minutes before it opened. We counted on staking our claim to the biggest washers because Doug, who collected the change, fixed the machines, and generally took care of the place, would often open up a little early for us. That morning, everything went as planned until we were folding clothes already dry, while waiting for the towels and denims, which needed another ten minutes.

Muskrat and I were people watching. River Coin–Op was the only laundry for miles around, and it filled quickly every day. As we folded our things, gossiped, ragged each other, and commented on assorted humans coming and going, we both noticed a luxury motor home pull in, driven by a graying, well-dressed man. We had never seen him before.

He got down from the cab, went around to the other side, hauled in some pillowcases stuffed with laundry, returned for another load.

He didn't even pause in the doorway to assess the people at work, but catching sight of us, made a beeline through the crowd, as if we were old friends, as if we had an appointment. He stopped at the table where we were standing.

"Ladies," he addressed us in courtly style with a slight bow, "I have a problem. My wife has become ill, and I have had to take her to the hospital. It may seem incredible, but until today I've never done laundry in my life. She spoiled me, I guess. Tomorrow she's going to be released, and I want to get these"—he gestured toward the stuffed pillow-cases—"washed so she'll have a clean bed to come back to. I haven't the faintest notion how to go about it. Could you possibly show me?"

I looked at Muskrat, who is about twenty years older than I am, and one of the most matter-of-fact, motherly people I know. To my horror, she looked at me and sweetly replied, "I know Maggie will help you."

How could she betray me like that?

I was cornered. There was no way out. My laundry was done, I was all talked out, ready to go home, back to my canyon solitude. My pleasant vacant interval suddenly was full of this man and his dirty laundry.

I glanced desperately around. Over in the corner was a bank of washers where we could have lessons unobserved.

We dragged his laundry over there. I began explaining about fabrics, temperature, color. His supplies of soap and bleach were hopelessly inadequate, so I gave him mine.

As we began to work, he told me he was from Palm Desert, which explained the fancy motor home and lack of laundry experience. And without a trace of self-pity, he told me a little of his disappointment over the ruined plans for months of careless leisure.

By the time we got to this part of his story, I was digging down into one of those king-sized pillowcases.

I am proud of my Celtic heritage. I pride myself on remaining clearheaded in crises of the more dramatic sort. Some people have even accused me of creating crises so I can function well in them.

I don't faint at the sight of blood. I don't panic fighting a grass fire. I have wiped many baby bottoms, mucked hundreds of stalls, cleaned chicken houses.

But I have limits. There are some odors that really get to me.

My stomach told me even before my nose.

As I reached down into the pillowcase and pulled out the first sheet, the fetid stench of putrefying sickness and urine enveloped me. I stuffed the still-damp sheet into the washer as casually as I could. My little discourse on the mysteries of coin-op laundries faltered as I struggled to keep from throwing up.

My gracious companion kept his side of the conversation going as if he were entertaining me over a glass of vintage wine in his elegant living room, all the while continuing to work, putting his share of the odoriferous burden into another washer. Never did technology seem more welcome—or more inadequate.

As we persevered with our nauseating task, I became preoccupied with just one thing: to stifle my retching. Somehow I continued to talk, got machines started, showed him how to judge soap levels, described the drier process. I demonstrated the vending machine that exchanged dollar bills for dimes and quarters, and left him with some sheets of fabric softener, hoping the scent would cover any smell the washers couldn't get out.

My onerous duty done, trying not to run, I collected my laundry, Muskrat, and scuttled for the door. We glanced at our elderly friend and saw with relief that he'd struck up a conversation with a familiar denizen, a man about his own age.

I yanked open the door of the old heap someone in the parish had donated as a method of unloading a white elephant (literally: the car was white, elephantine, and guzzled gas like a mammoth at an oasis in the Sahara), pushed Muskrat and laundry sacks inside with equal force, and gunned the engine.

Before I could peel out, the man came to the door, waving my box of soap. I waved back and started driving. My stomach was somewhere near my vocal cords.

As I fought to drive and not to barf, I became aware of an odd sensation creeping toward the surface of awareness, but I pushed it down to confront Muskrat.

"Why did you do that? Why did you shove him off on me?"

Muskrat (who once ran a laundry) got an injured look on her face.

"Well," she purred, snuggling into her triumphant smugness, "you have more experience with those machines."

I was too flabbergasted at this outrageous untruth to respond.

I changed tacks.

"I feel sick."

"I bet," was Muskrat's riposte, smiling to herself.

The sensation I had pushed aside became insistent. Goose bumps popped out all over.

The face of the man with the appalling laundry hung suspended in the middle of the windshield. I wondered if I would have to stop the car. The preternatural something was beating at my inner door, trying to remind me of . . . of . . .

The image of the man with the laundry became the image of a leper.

Then it hit.

The heroism was all on the leper's side. The leper's embrace was so complete that Francis was compelled to return it. He embraced the leper and, in him, the whole world.

Maybe the leper was doing his laundry.

When I got home I wept, real tears.

I never forgot the man's dignity, his acceptance of his unfamiliar burden, his humility in asking for and accepting my ungenerous help. It was his graciousness that enabled me to do what little I did.

He helped me to forget myself in the struggle not to urp into the mess. He exposed my fastidiousness and my pride: if it had been me and my laundry, I'd probably have taken it to the dump or burned it before I would have submitted to such an ordeal, or else I'd have apologized the whole time, just making matters worse.

Even now as I look back, my flesh crawls: it was as if he was expecting to find us there.

It isn't every day that contemplation comes in a laundry, though I suspect we miss by our own blindness more gifts than we can imagine.

I shared all this with Muskrat, who chortled in a knowing way, claiming she didn't understand a word of it. The laundry affair wasn't the first or last time she revealed herself as a desert mother.

For all of that, I still hate to do laundry. I grudge every moment in a coin-op, and I'm just as selfish when I get there.

But there is also a nagging feeling that perhaps all is not quite what it was. Deep down I wonder whether I will ever again see the divine Face, not through ecstatic contemplation, or perfect monastic observance, or splendid liturgy, or profound silence, but through what may be the only means I can see and yet live: in a sack of dirty laundry.

And as I write I see, suddenly, that I missed the most significant clue of all: the tears I shed that day were the first outward sign of medicinal anointing.

The Storm

By the end of my first summer in Hunter I was wound tight as a clock spring. In June, the bulldozers had come up the creek to shove the gravel around. The old stagecoach road no longer dead-ended at my cabin. You could drive through to town—if you wanted to take the risk.

Now I was plagued by joyriders.

Every leaf and flower was coated with dust flung into the atmosphere by their pickups and dirt bikes. Most came by day, but the night riders were the worst. You could hear them careening around curves, barely avoiding oblivion. The trespasser problem became intolerable. Weekends left Hunter residents exhausted, whether they were aggressors or defenders.

It seemed incredible that the county insisted on opening this road to the public through one of the least accessible and driest areas in the state. It was too dangerous to attract anyone but thrill-seekers or troublemakers. With August came hunting season, and what had seemed stupidity became insanity.

Fires could be ignited by stray bullets, careless campers, a car exhaust pipe in dry grass, the sun prismed through broken glass. One monumental fire that came close to incinerating Hunter was started by a spark from a lawn mower. Even splitting wood could be dangerous, and I shuddered at the sparks that fell from metal striking metal as I heaved the sledge above my head and brought it down on the wedge disappearing into the wood.

Splitting wood helped the tension. I developed a jungle alertness I'd not had since I lived in Manhattan, an undercurrent of fear that made me jump at every snapped twig.

The dogs were nervous, too. Even the *plop!* of a kingfisher dropping like a child-thrown rock into one of the quiet pools of the now slowly moving creek would set them barking.

Each time we heard a shot, Kelly quivered and slunk to me, crowding my legs. At night we could hear poachers, and sometimes see their lights. If they got close enough, I'd phone the sheriff.

Leticia's son brought his arsenal of rifles and pistols to shoot targets in the dry creekbed between our houses. But the real stress came from living deep in standing timber that could ignite from spontaneous combustion. Smoke became an obsession.

Since I was late with my woodpile, I would work on it every morning before it got too hot. I was splitting bay, a tortuous, enervating job because it grows beveled; the teeth in the grain are loath to part. Bay burns hot and long when dry, but you have to split it a year ahead, expose it to the sun, keep it covered through a winter in order to season it. When you finally pry a section apart, the aromatic oil is overpowering.

The bay is a paradoxical tree. Fire will spread rapidly enough in a fir forest, but the bays interspersed among the firs become living torches. Bay will grow only where there is water, but it converts that water to resin dry weather renders volatile. I'd seen bays literally explode from the heat of nearby flames, trunks and upraised branches become arcing pillars of fire roaring through the canopy with the force of rocket engines.

The Boy Scouts routinely set their camp on fire. Since they were just across the creek and slightly down the west fork from Leticia, the smell of their bonfires would come upstream with the evening breeze. Sometimes I would phone Muskrat, and sometimes she would phone me.

"Do you smell smoke?"

"No. Can you tell where it's coming from?"

"I'll have a look around and phone you back."

One night I heard motorcycles stop on the crossing. I never went out after trespassers at night, but I did have a big light with a long beam I could shine around the woods. Often that was enough to make people go away.

But I didn't mess with bikers. There wasn't much noise after this pair stopped, just an occasional quiet voice. Then silence. About 4:30 in the morning they revved up and left, the hogs' engines growling and reverberating off the canyon walls. They must have been audible clear down to Leticia's; they woke Muskrat up on the ridge.

I had been up all night, was relieved when they left. But I had a worse fright at dawn when I took the dogs to the crossing. In the long, dry grass, matted and broken by the bodies that had lain there, marijuana butts were smoldering.

Worst of all was the day some maniac raced through the woods throwing lighted firecrackers from his lurching red sports car. The deputies got him. But I waited three years until they nailed some spotlighters who had been foolish enough to turn around by my gate.

The dogs woke me. I watched as headlights, too low to be Tony's, came slowly across the stream and up to the entrance. The hatchback turned, exposing bright lights at the back. Inside, in a welter of bottles and cans, sat men and guns. Their technique, when they found a deer, was to dazzle it by shining a lamp in its eyes, then shoot for "sport" while it was blind and immobile.

As soon as the car started back down the crossing, I was on the phone to the sheriff. I'd been through this routine without result so many times by now that it hardly seemed worth the effort. Just as the call ended, I heard a shot. I rang back again. This time the deputy was excited.

"We have a car over that way. They found the bastards just as they fired that shot. Keep your eyes open for a wounded deer."

Spotlighting deer was sickening enough, but worse was the inept aim of careless hunters who wounded but didn't kill, who were too lazy to follow the animal through the brush to finish it off. Disabled deer seek water, and even if they make it as far as a stream, they die slowly from thirst, pain, loss of blood. The stream then remains polluted until the vultures, coyotes, and foxes clean up the carcass, and the rains come to wash the channel clean.

Next day, Keith, the game warden, stopped by. Together we searched the area where I thought I'd heard the shot. After dealing with trespassers, we'd become good friends.

"Never can thank you enough for those winter gates."

"Don't see how we could have survived without them."

But we didn't find the deer.

Getting the county to put gates on the ridges that first summer was one fight I'd enjoyed.

By the end of July, I knew I couldn't take the pressure from trespassers more than a few months a year. In winter, when the road ended at my gate, it was especially dangerous, and since the canyon contained nothing but posted land, no one had any reason to be down there.

I started bombarding the road department and the county supervisor's office with letters and phone calls. I talked to George, to Keith, to the deputies, to the neighbors. They all agreed the road should be closed formally by a barrier on top of the ridges, instead of informally by the creek in front of my cabin. We finally badgered our county supervisor into coming for a meeting.

Expecting hicks he could patronize, he was surprised to find uniforms from state and county services, as well as neighbors jammed in a tight circle around my tiny living space. They were sitting stiffly on the chairs I'd brought up from the LSD castle, sipping coffee and eating muffins.

I wore my formal white and brown habit, which none of the neighbors had ever seen, and in spite of all we'd been through together, it had the effect of a bucket of cold creek water on a barbecue. Even Muskrat was subdued.

The chunky, balding supervisor was late, as usual. He liked to make grand entrances. He offered the excuse of the condition of the roads, a remark that incited jeering hoots.

I began to be optimistic. This man thought he was dealing with dolts. True to political type, he tried, at first, to establish himself as a regular guy. He turned to me and said, har har, that women living alone usually took in a man for protection.

Everyone sniggered.

That was his second mistake.

After a psychological pause, I answered demurely, peeping out from under my veil, "In my position, that's hardly possible."

There was loud and raucous laughter. The supervisor's opening gambit had lost the game. His shiny pink pate reddened slowly to bright fuchsia. I knew we had our gates. But he wasn't giving up without a fight.

He asked for comments, and found he was facing a unanimous, well informed, articulate, angry, politically influential group. But he still thought I was the weak link. In spite of my letters and phone calls, my reminders of county liability, he saw not a person, but the habit.

After everyone had spoken, he tried me again.

"Tell me about a typical encounter with a trespasser. I don't believe you're in as much danger as you suggest."

I exchanged looks with the deputy, who shifted in his chair and ducked his head in order to examine the crease in his trousers at closer range, and with Keith, who sat deadpan across the circle. I could only hope they would control their laughter until I made the *coup de grâce*. I began to talk in a docile, soft, nunlike voice, gazing into the middle distance, thinking of Audrey Hepburn.

"I follow the procedure the deputies have suggested. When I see people are going to trespass, I ask them politely not to. When they begin to trespass, I ask them again, more firmly. At this point they usually respond with a lot of filth. No one should have to put up with that every day of their lives. When they make threats, I take their license numbers and phone the sheriff.''

The deputy nodded in confirmation.

The supervisor, having walked into the trap, then took the bait. I heard the door clang behind him, the coveted gates click shut, the padlocks snap as the pins were pushed home.

"What do you mean by filth no one should have to listen to?''

There was a long silence. I dared not look at Muskrat. When the tension reached the breaking point, I faced the supervisor, blinking innocently from the safety of my white coif, and, in a sweet neutral voice, let fly.

Muskrat's hand, clutching a bit of muffin, stopped in midair, halfway to her mouth.

The deputy looked up from the speck on his trousers and stared. Leticia's jaw dropped. I lowered my eyes, put my hands under my scapular, and managed to blush.

"Well, er, hum, yes,'' coughed the supervisor, rising out of his chair as if he'd suddenly discovered he was sitting in poison oak. "I'll speak to the public works department today, and we'll have those gates in by the rains. George, you give Glen Stone a ring and tell him what you want. . . .''

Everyone else got up, talking all at once, bumping into one another as they made for the door. The deputy twinkled at me as he followed the supervisor outside. The volunteer fire chief shook his head and grinned, holding himself firmly in check. Only Keith and Muskrat stayed behind.

"Those gates are going to make my job a hell of a lot easier.''

"Thanks for coming. Your presence helped a lot.''

After he left, Muskrat was more blunt.

"*Where* did you hear that?''

"I told you. I've been telling you all summer. It's the sort of abuse every trespasser dishes out.''

"What possessed you . . .''

"He asked, didn't he?''

Muskrat considered this. Then her face began to crumple like the side of the scarp when rock begins to move.

Unable to control myself a moment longer, I joined her, convulsed, until the tears were pouring down my cheeks.

When we'd wiped our eyes, she said, "Let's go over to the ocean to celebrate before the phone starts ringin'."

The gossip machine would be running full bore after news of the meeting went out over village CBs.

Going to the ocean was the way we celebrated the small daily triumphs and mourned the tragedies of our lives. We'd travel out of Hunter through Pneumonia Gulch to the main highway along the river, and turn west. Halfway to the coast, we'd stop at a general store for imported beer and stone-ground wheat crackers.

In twenty minutes we'd be on a high cliff overlooking the river's end and the Pacific. The immense conflicting forces of fresh water flowing out and salt tides flowing in continually shifted the sand and gravel, moving the mouth north or south, sometimes gradually, sometimes overnight.

When the mouth is open, steelhead and salmon enter to spawn. Seals and sea lions hunt them, flopping into the sea from their rookery on the beach. Pelicans fold their wings making kamikaze dives to get their share, punctuating the blue-gray-green water with white splashes, controlled crashes that thrust the birds below the surface, only to bob up with a pouch full of squirming prey. Waiting for the pelican to surface is the tax collector, an attendant gull that snatches at scraps, sometimes bold enough to yank on a scaly tail hanging out of the pelican's beak.

The color of the water is never the same. The mood of the coastline ranges from halcyon, when surf barely laps the broad sandy apron below the jetty, to waves forty feet high that crash majestically across the bars, creating one vast, boiling maelstrom. Down the coast, a rock more than a hundred feet high juts into the ocean, and we judge the roughness of the waters by the height of spray smashing against it.

Rosinda ©

On calm days the ocean's hue ranges from electric blue to azure. When the action of the water digs out a deep lagoon but keeps the mouth to one side, and if the sun is at the right angle, we can watch fish swimming in the clear water, and seals chasing them. After storms, though, the freshwater flood is loaded with reddish yellow silt carrying tree trunks, dead livestock, and entire houses.

Where this violent stream meets the more furious ocean depends on the moment you arrive. If the storm is at its peak (and you risk your life to drive), the mouth of the river all but disappears under gigantic waves cascading over the muddy waters that pour beneath them. If things have calmed down a bit, the tea-colored river may have spread as far as a mile out to sea.

We loved this view in all weathers and seasons. In spring, seals gather on the sand spit, fat from feasting, waiting for their pups to be born. There are always a few rollicking in the surf, but the majority lie together in lines along the bars and the edge of the channel where it meets the

ocean. Slugs, Muskrat calls them, and they do look like fat gray mollusks lolling in the sunshine, raising their heads only to aim territorial feints at each other, or to turn their heavy bodies to expose another surface to the sun, or to scoop sand over themselves with languorous flippers.

Summers we didn't go to the ocean so much: too many tourists, too much to keep an eye on at home. But when autumn and the pelicans came, or in winter, when the gray whales migrated, we'd go almost daily to watch the antics of the big gray-brown birds and their feisty gull companions, or to look for spouts that marked the progress of the leviathans moving south from the Arctic to Baja and Scammons Lagoon, where they give birth to their calves.

In my first months, I had tried to avoid leaving the canyon. But as time passed, its narrowness began to close in on me. The demons gibbered and cackled; flashbacks made study and prayer impossible; the concentration required by weaving became intolerable.

In the past, color flowing through my hands as I put a warp on the small table loom set up on the porch would have been enough to still them. But the tedious, hypnotic tasks of threading heddles or throwing the shuttle created in me a space, a battleground, where openness and humiliation wrestled in mortal combat. I was not unaware of the desert counsel to sit in the cell, but I also knew there was hubris in the illusion of self-sufficiency.

Muskrat had a sixth sense for knowing when I needed to get out of there, to seek infinite perspective from the turnout on the cliff. And there was volatile Eddie, the son of Portuguese immigrants. His cultural chauvinism sometimes made emotional demands that exhausted even the resources of her stalwart Indian-English-Jewish ancestry, and the hard training of her childhood.

Muskrat had her own demons. They haunted her memories, insistent mental images that came unsummoned, thwarting all efforts to make them go away: a childhood blotted by her father's early death and a mother's wanderings from one migrant labor camp to another; the humiliation of being penniless and barefoot in Hunter, a stigma she still feels in the provincial, haughty attitude of a few families; her first husband lying dead beside the gun he'd used to shoot himself; a birthing without joy or a single cry released from the still center of hell in a whirlpool of pain; a father-in-law's contempt that bypassed her in his will so that she was her son's guest on the ranch rightly hers; the twisted, sometimes abused bodies and damaged minds of her former charges; the terror of her pickup hurtling through the air after a drunk hit her; the effects of the head injury from which she would never quite recover. . . .

To hear her daily concerns made my own seem petty. I'd finally, haltingly, told her some of my history, remained reticent about the rest. But she knew my deep conflict from within, and she was a healer.

September wound us so tight that the air seemed to swarm with silent voices screaming.

First there was Labor Day weekend, a holiday some people celebrate as if they feel they will never have another chance for booze, risks, and outrageous behavior. Only the international con game called Christmas can surpass it in terms of the physical and emotional abuse generated by wishful projection of the ultimate good time. The main difference is that at Christmas it would have been raining for several months. This particular September was so hot and dry that looking cross-eyed would spark combustion.

We gritted our teeth and held on, phoning each other at the slightest unusual noise. I heard a shot from Leticia's on Friday afternoon, even though she'd told me her son and grandson already had their bucks. I phoned Muskrat to come and keep an eye on things.

I ran downstream along the creekbank, splashed across the shallows, trotted beside Leticia's pasture fence until I came to the paddock gate. I called our musical code just in case she had been after trespassers, but before her answer reached me through the high-pitched barking of her sheep-dogs, I ran up against death.

There in the track, with a neat bullet hole just behind his shoulder, lay a white wolf.

Leticia's voice broke through my shock. Her straight, slim figure came into sight on the path curving from her house.

"No-good people let their dogs run loose," she said in everyday tones, "this un's bin runnin' with another—he got away—and they wuz chasin' the horses an' killed two goats. Where in the heck d'ya figger this critter came from?"

"It's a wolf."

"I know it's a wolf, but it ain't like no wolf that's ever bin seen in these parts."

"It's a Siberian wolf. People breed them for pets."

"They *what?*"

"They breed them for pets. It's the latest fashion."

Leticia gave me one of her "the world is even crazier than I thought" looks and said, "Yeah, an' then they bring 'em up here for the weekend an' let 'em run loose an' people lose their stock. Well," she nudged the body with her toe, "this 'un won't bother nobody again. I hated to do it . . ."

I looked up. Tears were pouring down her face.

". . . but I didn't have no choice. . . . You got time for a cup of tea?"

"Muskrat's watching my place, so I've got to get back. She's got weirdos of her own to fend off."

"I'll walk a ways with you, then."

That night a small group of people came to stay at the LSD castle. They were middle-class and responsible, and while I was glad to have someone else around in case of emergency, it made the fire danger all the greater. One spark from the barbecue, one overturned lantern, kids hiding lighted candles . . .

Saturday's main event was also downstream, and began with the sounds of a guerrilla war. Poor Kelly nearly went out of his mind. Because of the group at the LSD castle, I didn't bother Muskrat.

Below our property line the stream widened into broad, gravelly flats, almost too hot to touch at this time of year. Water still flowed sluggishly in the stream, but it hugged the western bank. On these flats, Alan, Leticia's grown son, his blond girlfriend, Alan's thirteen-year-old son, and a sallow rat-faced man, were having target practice. The target hung in the window of a derelict car, far gone to rust, that Alan had shoved into the bank in an effort to reduce erosion caused by gravel mining farther downstream.

I waited for a lull in the firing and shouted. They waved me on.

"That's one way to keep the trespassers off," I said, staring at the small munitions dump of rifles, shotguns, and pistols in Alan's old army jeep.

"Yeah," grunted Alan, looking down at me, his blond beard glinting in the shade thrown by his black Stetson. He wasn't much for conversation, and when his short emotional fuse was lit, you wanted to be a long, long way from the explosion.

Jeannie, his girlfriend, and Patrick, his son, said hello. The rat-faced man, who was holding a shotgun, slouched against the jeep, saying nothing.

"You shoot?"

"Only a rifle. I never hunted."

Alan was feeling hospitable. "Try this."

He picked up a .22 magnum by the barrel and held it out.

I'd never seen a pistol like it outside of Clint Eastwood posters. It would have been unneighborly to refuse what was, by country standards, a generous offer and a sign of trust.

But I had a problem. If I missed, it would be all over the county that I couldn't hit the broadside of an old car. If I aimed well, it would make me out to be a liar.

I sighed, and took the pistol. I tried to steady my jumpy nerves as I aimed along what I guessed was the sight, and adopted what I hoped was a reasonable stance.

No one said anything.

The pistol was the first—and, I hope, last—I'd ever held. I don't like guns much, though I'm not afraid of them. Yet I couldn't help admiring its elegant balance in my hands as I took a deep breath, let it out, held the exhalation, and squeezed the trigger.

A second shot went off before I could catch myself—the trigger was so smooth, and the gun fired almost without recoil. My muscles tensed as I put the magnum politely in Alan's outstretched hand.

He was studying the target.

"Not sure I hit anything," I babbled foolishly, "but I sure appreciate the chance to fire one of these."

I wanted to leave. Now.

Alan took me over to the car window. "These are yours," he growled, pointing near the center, looking as if he'd caught me stealing horses. "I thought you said you'd never fired a pistol before."

"I haven't," I replied, fighting to keep steady. "Beginner's luck."

It was obvious that Alan didn't believe me—he was suspicious by nature—but to say more would only make things worse.

I made my good-byes on the excuse of the busy weekend, and tramped off upstream, burdened by the guilt women bear when they succeed, however inadvertently.

If I had missed, Alan would have despised me for not being able to handle a gun. But having hit the target, I was now both suspect and a threat. A woman competent with guns could not easily be controlled. The old familiar feeling crept over me, and as soon as I was out of sight, I hunkered down by the stream until the water, slipping over stones, restored calm.

What if I had taken my neighbors' advice and accepted a gun? I'd always felt a weapon only escalated hostilities— aside from mistrusting my temper. The killing machine worked lightly, easily, taking life without thought or effort.

Muskrat, informed by her third ear, was sitting on the porch comforting Kelly when I got back.

"What happened?"

I told her.

She didn't say anything.

I wondered if she was thinking of the bitter morning when she'd come out of her house to find her husband's body after he'd shot himself. "It was so strange," she'd say, shivering, when she needed to talk about it. "I knew he was dead, but all I could think about was how cold it was, an' I had to get a blanket on him."

I changed the subject.

"You hear a weather forecast?"

"Nope, but nothin's comin' yet. Rod's up for the weekend. He's brought his horses an' a new girlfriend."

Rod was a Vietnam veteran, her son. He'd become an R.N. and worked in a hospital emergency room.

"You like her?"

"Not especially, but they're havin' theirselves a good time. Said they might ride down to see you. Eddie got a wild pig last evenin', an' is hopin' for a buck. There's been a big one on the hill these past few evenin's, but he's always been somewhere's else. Now I gotta get back, 'cause he's up on the roof sealin' it, an' hasn't the sense God gave a goose to come down out of the sun. Here, I brought you somethin'."

She handed me a package of fresh pig liver.

"By the way," she started the engine of her yellow Subaru, "I don't want to alarm you, but there's a fire up north. Some of our people have gone off to help. Yell if you get problems."

Thanks a bunch. News of a fire is all I need. . . .

. . . as I ran out to deal with yet another drunk who had come down to the crossing from the other side and stopped his blue pickup in the middle.

After an ostentatious pee in the creek, ignoring the "No Trespassing" signs plastered on every tree, he started into our woods.

The dogs were already barking. Kelly was putting on his best display, leaping and snarling at the end of his chain at the bottom of the steps. He couldn't be trusted not to jump over the porch gate. Pomo was baying, pushing her nose through the slats, her tail seeming to lever force into each new effort.

"Bark!" I shouted over my shoulder to encourage them. They redoubled their efforts as I ran for the promontory on the old bridge abutment overlooking the dam. . . .

≈≈≈

We got through the weekend, but there was no letup in the cumulative tension. The gates were in; we had only to wait for the first big storm for George to close them. It couldn't happen soon enough. But if the rains were late. . . .

Our hopes were pinned on the equinox.

Every year I had lived in this part of the world, the equinox brought moisture. When I was growing grapes, I prayed it would be no more than a phalanx of white, gray, and black clouds that would moisten the ripening clusters with enough drizzle to plump them before harvest, not measurable rainfall, which would ruin the crop.

I now found myself praying for a deluge. We couldn't continue like this. Something would happen to strain us beyond tolerance, something trivial, something unknown. . . .

The fire up north grew worse. In a few days we could smell smoke, carried on a hot wind. Everyone was restless. The wild things hid during the pounding heat, but were out at night, scrabbling, rustling, creeping, stalking. The tributaries were dry, and while both forks of Foxfire were still running, the water level had dropped to a trickle at the bottom of the streambed.

Creatures that normally got their water from the side creeks startled one another as they crept from cover to cross the exposed gravel to drink. In the morning we could read the tracks of otter and raccoon, 'possum and deer. Coyotes wailed at the waxing moon, causing the dogs to go berserk, and once a mountain lion screamed across from the cabin, the shock wave recharging the silence.

I couldn't sleep, and neither could the dogs. After a few hours of tossing on my mat in the loft, I'd give up, leash them, walk the road illumined by starlight filtering through the trees and glaucous luminescence from weed clumps on the bank.

I walked quietly, expectantly; the dogs paced solemnly beside me, ears twitching.

Sometimes an owl would call, or swoop upward on silent feathers, surprised at its kill by our footsteps. Once we were frozen by the unnaturally loud chatter of a rattlesnake—until we realized it was in the culvert below us, its sound magnified by the hollow metal drum.

Finally we would reach the top of the ridge, blinking

under the vast dome of heaven, free from the crowding trees. The stars that had winked through the canopy now poured on us their cold fire.

You wrap yourself with light as with a cloak, and spread out the heavens like a curtain.

Here, far from city lights, they shone resplendent with subtle hues: dirty red giants; dazzling white newborns; fuzzy cloud nebulae; stars circling stars in endless perspective, everywhere the film of light from yet more stars, too faint for the naked eye.

Sometimes I'd bring binoculars to gaze more intimately at old friends, but mostly I stood and wondered, or listened to the hush that lay over the hamlet below, asleep under the shelter of the mountains. The dogs would sit beside me, quiet and alert, turning their heads at every rustle or chirp, ears pricked to the stars' whispered crackling, and after time uncounted, we'd rise, turn back into the tunnel of foliage, wind slowly down to the cabin.

Muskrat read the signs, or perhaps it was her uncanny hearing, or the strange acoustics of the mountain. "You went walkin' last night, didn't you? I saw your tracks. Did you know Kelly has a coyote's print?"

I marveled at her ability to pick out our signs from many others, and then remembered that I never had to catch my supper. Or sometimes she'd phone the next morning to say, "Why didn't you call an' tell me you were walkin' last night? I would of gone with you."

But she meant only to express concern. She knew I needed these solitary walks, the stars' seething caress.

When waiting became agony, Muskrat and I would head for the river's mouth to search the western horizon for weather signs. A sullen gauze hung over the coast, and we would argue whether or not we were seeing real clouds beyond the fair-weather summer fog bank hanging perpetually over the ocean a couple of miles out.

The fog sometimes spread inland in the early morning as far as Muskrat's ridge, but more often it blanketed the hamlet below. It was always a surprise, having left my sunny canyon, to plunge into the chill dankness that lingered over the village.

But there was no sign of rain.

Early one Saturday morning, needing the ocean's enigmatic immensity, I went alone to the coast.

At last.

Beyond the white barrier of fog, great masses of dark cloud were expanding.

All day I held that storm in hope and anticipation, fed it on longing, opened to its gathering around me.

Even so, by late afternoon, the sliver of sky over the canyon was still the same old fiery blue. I walked up the ridge to see what had happened to the storm.

Clouds frowned in the west, but along their black edge ran a line of bizarre, intensely white, almost fluorescent ones, whorled like thick cream whipped by an electric mixer.

Dread crawled up my scalp. I'd seen similar clouds only once before. They heralded the worst blow I'd ever been through. I was living outdoors, for the most part, 2,300 feet above the sea. Not understanding the formation, I was caught in a tent that night. It felt as if the gusts would scoop me up, a body in a nylon shroud, and fling me off the cliff into the sea.

I ran all the way home to phone Muskrat, wondering why she hadn't phoned me.

"Have you looked out the window lately?"

"No. I been makin' pies all day for Rachel's freezer. Hang on. . . . Weird lookin', aren't they?"

"Yeah. I think we're going to get wet."

"You're all wet anyway."

"Takes one to know one."

"Hey, how come you're not up here helpin' me with these pies?"

"You didn't ask."

"Ask? You're supposed to *know*." She muttered to keep the line open until we ran out of banter.

I was rushing to bring in firewood when light leached from the canyon, leaving the yellowing dusk and sullen muteness I remembered from my first visit. Rapidly lowering pressure electrified air already laced with the expectancy of living things waiting for moisture.

And me: I wanted not just rain but a torrential autumn storm that would end the fire danger, close the road, bring peace. Now that I had a roof over my head, I half hoped for a blow as bad as the one that nearly dumped me in the ocean, a tumult that would give voice to my inarticulate pain.

The last bilious light saw me running around checking windows and doors, hauling tarps over wood split and unsplit, anchoring them with logs and rocks. I brought in as much firewood as would fit into the space beside the stove, stacked more on the porch, covered it.

The dogs clung to my heels, hiding their nervousness by pretending to play hunt-the-mouse in one of the piles of short stove wood. Kelly picked up a piece and tossed it at my feet. Even in this sulphurous atmosphere, he wanted to play fetch.

Hope springs eternal in the canine breast. . . .

The first huge drops spattered the dry earth, raising little poofs of dust. We ran for the porch. The roof vibrated with rain as we dashed inside; soon it was roaring. I had never seen such rain.

But overwhelming was the scent released into the air by the forest as falling water washed dust from leaf pores, trunks, and stems, the incense of parched woodland reaching to the clouds, drinking its fill, slaking its desire, exhaling perfume into the atmosphere: fir, bay, madrone, sage, and coyote brush. Moisture always brought out this fragrance, but nothing in the year ever matched the sweet drink offering of the first rains.

Then the wind began.

The first gusts smacked into the cabin like a wet fish across the face. Leaves and twigs spiraled in the air and were carried horizontally for hundreds of feet. Plastered to the skylights, they changed pattern continually as rain sheeted

over the glass. It was as if we had taken refuge in the dark tube of a kaleidoscope.

Pomo lay in her cedar nest in front of the wood stove, head up and alert, listening with every fiber. Kelly flumped himself on the matting and put his lobo head on oversized feet. When the first big tree went down with the *crack!* of a Bunyan-sized 30–30, he crept over to huddle against me.

There was no point sitting without a light. It wasn't very cold, but I lit a fire against the damp and dark, and put the kettle on. We stared into the flames as the storm thundered through the canyon like a demon express. The cabin shuddered and rocked, straining on its piers, lashed by branches flung against walls and roof.

I was making coffee when the dogs leapt to their feet, barking. Impossible headlights came down the hill.

I quickly lit the large kerosene lamp. A familiar orange truck with a county seal pulled in the gate, and a yellow, oilcloth-wrapped figure sprinted for the porch.

The wind threw the door open as George tramped in.

"Sorry to drip all over your floor. This storm is going to take the crossing out, an' I wanted to check how bad it was."

He shut the door and propped against it. Water gathered in puddles under his feet. "Are you OK?"

"Yes, fine. How about cashing in that rain check?"

"Sure, but I can't stay long, 'cause the water's building up fast behind the dam—it's 'way too much for the culvert to handle."

I was already pouring coffee into a big plastic mug.

"Listen," George said as he took it, "if another truck comes down, tell 'em I've gone across, but say I said they shouldn't risk it."

"For God's sake, be careful."

"Thanks. Keep us in your prayers tonight." And he was gone into the storm.

Moments after George disappeared, above the tumult of slashing wind and rain, I heard a grinding clatter. The force of the rising stream had broken through the gravel barrier, dragging the steel culvert downstream against the bank. I was seized with wild joy. The gates would be closed. The second truck couldn't get across even if they decided to risk it.

A half hour later, the dogs announced visitors. I waved my big flashlight through the window. The second truck turned in, and two figures raced for the cabin, clumping onto the porch. By the time they reached the door, I had coffee poured. They were there less than a minute.

"Stay inside. Thanks for the coffee. We'll lock the gates." And they were gone.

In the small hours I jerked awake. The voice of the wind was rising from a roar to a demented shriek. The dogs jumped to their feet, barking hysterically as I began to climb down the ladder. Crockery chinked and clacked as the cabin lurched and swayed like a drunk on stilts.

I was thrown off the ladder to the floor.

Trees were falling all around; debris smashed against the walls and windows. The dogs staggered to where I lay stunned. After a moment, I was able to sit up. I put my arms around them and buried my head in Kelly's ruff.

The waters saw you, O God; the water saw you and trembled; the very depths were shaken.

The clouds poured out water; the skies thundered; your arrows flashed to and fro;

The sound of your thunder was in the whirlwind; your lightnings lit up the world; the earth trembled and shook.

Your way was in the sea, and your paths in the great waters, yet your footsteps were not seen. . . .

He parted the heavens and came down with a storm cloud under his feet.

He mounted on cherubim and flew, he swooped on the wings of the wind. He wrapped darkness about him; he made dark waters and thick clouds his pavilion.

From the brightness of his presence, though the clouds burst hailstones and coals of fire.

The Lord thundered out of heaven; the Most High uttered his voice. . . .

〜

By first light the wind had died back, but the thunderous noise went on.

The creek that had been a trickle was now a turbulent river. Brown water churned and sluiced and sucked against the far bank, carrying leaves, twigs, branches, whole trees. It covered the gravel, and was rising steadily on the cabin side.

The water pipe was suspended twenty feet above the channel between concrete abutments. I put on my boots and went to check.

The stream narrowed between the concrete walls. The backwash of water fighting to get through piled high into curving waves. On the downstream side, the constricting gate expelled the water in a savage flume. Within the gate, compression pushed the water level almost ten feet higher than the rest of the creek. A few feet more, and a floating tree would take the line out.

Water! I ran to the back of the cabin and pulled the fifty-pound sack of dog food from its clean thirty-gallon green garbage can, put the can on the porch, and filled it from the hose.

I slogged up the quagmire road alongside the fuming tributary. It was nearly impassable. Water ran down in sheets faster than the drainage ditches could carry it to the culverts, and axle-deep ruts crisscrossed the surface. Unless the road crew came, I'd have to fix it with a shovel by hand.

Trees lay every which way; some were blown against others, knocking them sideways, leaning at impossible angles. I stopped every few feet to haul branches to the road's edge and throw them down the embankment. When I rounded a curve halfway up, I saw that the tornado had picked up three enormous firs and twisted them around one another. The trunks were too big for my sixteen-inch chain saw, and the roots of one had eaten a hole out of the road's edge.

Phone cable lay here and there in spaghetti tangles.

I had some coins in my pocket, so I crawled over, around, under the broken trees to walk to Hunter, hoping the main lines were still intact. Under the rain's hiss was spooky silence; the devastated forest unnerved me.

The village too was so silent and still that its residents might have been spirited away. At the pay box outside the general store, I put calls in to George's answering machine at the county yard, and to the phone company.

The hike back up the scarp was cold, wet, and muddy.

Toward late afternoon, the dogs signaled visitors. It hardly seemed possible that the road crew would have cleared the trees so quickly, though the rain had slackened. Then two trail bikes with yellow-clad riders putt-putted down the hill, beeping merrily.

"We've come to rescue you," shouted Eddie, riding a serpentine around the debris on the ruined road, laughing his infectious, booming laugh.

Muskrat followed more cautiously. "What'd you have to go an' knock down them trees for," she accused me. "We had one heck of a time gettin' these bikes underneath!"

Their slickers were streaked with red mud.

"Yeah," Eddie chimed in, "we couldn't raise you on the phone, an' since this place is such a two-bit outfit, we thought we'd better come an' check. Man, what a storm! Just as we got the bikes on your side, the road crew came. We stayed to watch, or we'd o' been here sooner."

I thought of their mobile home exposed on the ridge, and George, who was as good as his word. "That's really great of you. Thanks! Did you have any trouble up there?"

"Naw." Eddie bit the word, pulling it to one side with his head, tearing it away from silence with his teeth. The furrows deepened in his square brown Portuguese face as he burst out laughing again. "We didn't have no trouble. You sure are lucky none o' them trees fell on you! Man, look at that creek!"

We went to check the water pipe. It had begun to slip its mooring and droop toward the rushing water. Together we pulled on it, leaning all our weight against the heavy, liquid-filled PVC, while Muskrat tightened the cable. The creek had dropped a bit, but the torrent was still scouring the concrete walls.

"Thanks," I said when we were finished. "Now do come in and have some coffee." Muskrat pulled some pastries out of her pannier, Eddie pulled a long black object out of his, and we went inside.

"Lissen," he ordered, shaking the water out of his salt-and-pepper hair, "there's a couple more storms backed up out there, an' you just dunno what's gonna happen. We brought you this here battery-powered CB just in case it'll work even with the ridge an' trees an' all between us."

He showed me how to use it, what channels to try, how to call.

"Up at the house we're Muskrat Base. That's our handle."

"Well," I laughed, "I guess that makes me Muskrat Ramble."

But it was Muskrat on whom the name stuck that day.

Next morning, a light blue telephone truck from our alternative utility stopped outside the gate. I ran through the rain to thank the crew for the prompt repair.

The red-bearded giant driving the rig winked and said, "Can't have you bein' out here cut off."

I knew then, if I hadn't before, that the community had accepted me.

~~~~

A couple of days later it was still raining. Everything in the cabin was beginning to smell like wet gym socks. When I couldn't stand it any longer, I phoned Muskrat, gathered up every item that would wash, and we went to the laundry.

There was hardly anyone there that day. After we'd put our clean, sweet-smelling clothes in Muskrat's car, by silent agreement we turned away from home and headed for the sea.

The river was in flood, due to crest about the same time as an extreme tide. We had about two hours before the peak. It was mammoth, brown and rolling fast. Every once in a while a log or branch would roil to the surface and disappear.

Before we reached the turn near the river's mouth, Muskrat spotted some sheep stranded on a point of land being taken by the water. She knew the owners, as she knows everyone in these hills, and we stopped at their house to tell the young wife. She thanked us, and raced for her gear.

"They do everything together with the sheep," Muskrat told me as we drove on, an unusual arrangement in that culturally traditional farming community.

We went to the beach this time, as close to the littoral as

we could get. We wanted to see the height of the waves from ground level. The rangers had shut off the road to our left where it was already falling into the sea. The moving mountains that were waves crossed and crashed and flung themselves against beach and boulder, sending spray high above us, higher than the hundred-foot outcrop to which the washed-out road had led.

The mouth of the river to our right was lost under the turmoil of water. Huge combers rolled in, forcing back the fresh water boiling down from the mountains. Rain blew horizontally from the ocean. The earth beneath us trembled before the power of the surf against the low bluff, and though we realized at any moment it could give way and drop us into the churning foam, we were transfixed.

The breakers of death rolled over me, and the torrents of oblivion made me afraid.

The cords of hell entangled me, and the snares of death were set for me.

I called upon the Lord in my distress and cried out to my God for help.

He heard my voice from his heavenly dwelling; my cry of anguish came to his ears.

Finally our time ran out, and we started back. On the way, we saw Muskrat's friend climbing precariously sideways along the fenceline on the flooded river flat toward the stranded sheep, putting one boot in a square wire opening, bringing the other up beside it. We stopped in case she needed help. She began to shout at someone standing on the other bank of the immense expanding river. We saw a car start up, and she waved us off.

We barely got past the low place on the road; water was already creeping over its surface.

The damage reports starting coming in on the radio. It was the first year since 1866 that two hard winters had come one on the other. Perhaps this was why the settlers, lulled by beauty and the even-tempered climate, built too close to the sleeping sea, or in deceptively lovely meadows, which were dried-up lakes. We traded stories we'd heard at the Hunter post office, laughing over local characters competing for glory, and their exaggeration.

Then we fell silent.

I pondered imponderables: the power and majesty of the storm; the kindness of people; the towering surf; the tragedy of battered homes and lost lives.

The storm was not evil of itself, and the extravagance of people who risk everything to live near earth's loveliness is greater than pride that ignores the elements. It will be the same when the long overdue 9 Richter earthquake comes: buildings will be destroyed, lives lost, history repeated. But is it human hubris that builds on faults, or is it the folly of being held in thrall by the splendor of the marriage feast where earth is wedded to heaven and the sea?

During the bad weather I'd been reading Steinbeck's *Log from the Sea of Cortez*. With his friend Ed Ricketts, Steinbeck went on a marine biology collecting trip in the Gulf of California. He asked questions in 1940 we are still asking more than half a century later, but with higher stakes. His sense of telescoping time and urgency is ours.

We were making the turn to Hunter, when a line came back to me that seemed to sum up all that we had seen and experienced in recent days: "Faced with all things," Steinbeck wrote of Darwin's explorations in the same area, "he cannot hurry."

So it is with us: the storm, the kindness, the beauty, the terrible price, the resurrecting spirit. People will build on the coast again, though the coast is changing beyond recognition; people will build on faults; people will live in the flooded meadows.

The quiet beauty, the terrible beauty, the many-faceted beauty will not let us hurry, will not let us go. It is a living mirror of the Love that sustains the whole fabric at every moment: rocks and waves, trees and swift streams, wind— and the rain lashing my window this night many thousands of miles away, as another storm gathers me to its heart.

II

Seasons of Death and Life

October

The leaves fall from my fingers.
Cornflowers scatter across the field like stars,
                              like smoke stars,
By the train tracks, the leaves in a drift

Under the slow clouds
                    and the nine steps to heaven,
The light falling in great sheets through the trees,
Sheets almost tangible.

The transfiguration will start like this, I think,
                              breathless,
Quick blade through the trees,
Something with red colors falling away from my hands,

The air beginning to go cold. . .
                    And when it does
I'll rise from this tired body, a blood-knot of light,
Ready to take the darkness in.

—Or for the wind to come
And carry me, bone by bone, through the sky,
Its wafer a burn on my tongue,
                    its wine deep forgetfulness.

                              —*Charles Wright*

Eddie and the
Yellow Peril

Winters in Hunter are not solid rain from beginning to end, dull days and nights succeeding one on another. Indian summer is followed by more rain, but there are breaks between storms, sometimes weeks, sometimes a single brilliant day. Spring takes her time, a languid northward progress. She sends restless energy ahead of her.

It was just as well that there were gaps between storms, for when the weather closed in, so did the interior battle I continued to fight. During one of these bright intervals, I laid aside my struggle and phoned Muskrat.

"Howdy!" Muskrat sounded breathless.

"Muskrat? Lets get out of here."

"Sounds great. When . . ."

There was mumbling; the phone bump-thumped to the floor, and was retrieved. Eddie's voice came over the wire. He was out of breath, too.

"Maggie?"

"Eddie! What's happening?"

"I'm *coaxin'* her!"

"I think I phoned at the wrong time. Have fun!"

I hung up, laughing.

I went to the coast by myself. The sun was hot as early summer. A cool breeze laced the warmth; the lazy sea lapped at the beach, a blue cat drinking cream. The coast shimmered in stillness: birds motionless, basking in the heat; slugs lying inert along the sandbars, an occasional sleek body in the water, light reflecting off its slow porpoising. With these peaceful promises, I began my second year in Hunter.

Next morning, the phone rang.

"Mornin'," I answered, Hunter style.

"Let's get out of here."

Mischief got the upper hand.

"Did you have a good time?"

I don't know how a blush gets communicated over the phone, but somehow this one did.

"Shaddap. You're terrible. I thought you wuz supposed to be a nun."

"So I am. That doesn't mean I can't enjoy your high-jinks."

She refused to bite. "Let's get out of here."

"Fine by me. What did you have in mind, China?"

"No, you turkey . . ."

"We ate the turkeys."

"Not all of 'em, 'cause I'm talkin' to one. Anyway, it's an insult to turkeys."

I sputtered.

"Now hesh up and lissen. Let's go to the beach."

"This is starting to sound like a broken record."

"Not the overlook, dummy; let's go to the beach an' take a picnic. Let's make a day of it. Eddie wants to go, too."

Eddie was a retired engineer from a big fish warehouse in the city. That meant he could repair anything, and if he needed something that didn't exist, he would invent it. His devices were ingenious, from his prototype wind machine, which he built long before they were commercially available, to his car-servicing arrangement.

His friends and relations were always badgering him with things that needed fixing. When I'd finally been able to buy a generator, he patiently taught me to clean it. But he always had so many projects working that he never had time to do anything with us, and his cultural chauvinism made him dismiss our outings as boring hen parties. If he wanted to come along, this was real news.

Muskrat and I went to town to buy supplies. On the way back up the scarp, I asked her about the tremendous racket in the woods on the ridge south of her place.

"It's been goin' on some days now," she answered. "I dunno what Dan's doin' over there."

Dan owned many of the eighteen-wheelers that tore through the village, hauling logs and gravel. He collected heavy equipment the way small boys collect matchbox models.

We picked Eddie up and horsed around on the way back down. We were like grade-school children, unexpectedly released from classes. We stopped at the post office, and I went in to get our mail.

Carrie, the tall, pale postmistress, overheard all of Hunter's gossip. She had to know how to keep her mouth shut if she valued her life. But underneath her statuesque Our-Lady-Dying-of-Consumption exterior lay a wicked sense of humor.

I yanked wads of mail out of both boxes while saying hello. "What's all the commotion on the ridge?"

"Oh," smirked Carrie, her virginal smile somewhat marred by the canary feathers clinging to her lips, "don't you know? That's Dan's cathouse going up."

She waited until my laughter died away, and without missing a beat, covered her tracks. "He's going to store his heavy equipment up there."

Muskrat and Eddie had been watching through the plate-glass window; they wanted in on the joke.

"Whoa! Whew!" Eddie sang out as we backed away from the building. "The party's gettin' rough!"

When we reached the ocean we drove south, threading the green bluffs dotted with sheep. The coast spread before us, a scalloped necklace. Rocks off shore were dark jewels set in loops of seed-pearl froth on aquamarine.

Yesterday's same small waves plashed gently along the beaches. The air was crisp and clear as I'd ever seen it. Light, reflecting off the water, radiated through everything, and in spite of the cold wind, it was already hot enough to peel off jackets and sweaters.

We dickered briefly over which cove to picnic in, and decided on Portuguese Beach in honor of Eddie. When we opened the back and he saw all the sacks, he hollered, "Who's gonna pack all that stuff down the cliff? My God, you'd think you women were gonna stay here a week!"

But not to be outdone as Muskrat and I set off down the steep path with the heavy cooler between us, he grabbed blankets, beer, the few remaining paper bags, and trailed along behind. Except for a family clustered against the far cliff, we had the beach to ourselves. We found a spot out of the wind, and spread our blankets for the feast.

It was harmless enough: baloney sandwiches, ham sandwiches, chips, dips, celery sticks, chocolate chip cookies, lots of beer—all the usual picnic stuff. So utterly commonplace, the three of us sitting there, razzing each other, telling dumb jokes, laughing, falling into silence, basking in the heat, getting up now and again to wade the clear tide pools, exclaiming over starfish, urchins, fan polyps, anemones, barnacles, coralline algae in all their subtle colors and forms. The three of us, usually so driven, careless now of our many self-important responsibilities, flopped on backs and stomachs just like the seals farther up the coast, soaking in sunlight.

Oh, it was like any day at the beach, but not. It was unplanned, purposeless, leisured with true blessed leisure. We were spellbound by magical surf, greedy gulls, shiny rocks, icy water, three humans having a good time untrammeled by intention, reveling in the surprise of our own ordinariness.

The extraordinariness of it didn't hit us until we became aware that the sun was sinking. Bewildered by time's passage, we slipped on our jackets and began to collect the debris.

We trudged up the cliff to the car, and sat watching the great orange penny drop into the wine-dark slot; we drove silently north toward home through purple shadows along the shore.

We did not know it was the last such day we would ever have.

Not long after our idyllic picnic, Muskrat's anxiety intruded into one of our morning phone calls.

"Eddie's sick."

Muskrat could be a worrywart, but there was a note of concern in her voice that had nothing to do with professional medical hypochondria, or her need for attention.

"What's wrong?"

"I don't rightly know."

This really was alarming. Muskrat usually had a diagnosis ready to hand, or at least a firm opinion.

"I can't put my finger on it. He's had a cold-like, he's short of breath an' tired. It isn't like him. An' sometimes I think he's actin' funny, though I can't say how, exactly."

"Have you called the doctor?"

"Oh, you know, it's always the same damn thing with these health programs. If it isn't an emergency, it takes a month for an appointment."

"Make it an emergency."

"Well, I would, but what if it becomes one?"

"Yeah, you have a point. What are you going to do?"

"Ride it out, I guess. If he gets any worse, I'll phone again."

"How is Eddie taking it?"

"Oh, he's cantankerous as always, but I can tell he don't feel right."

When the doctor finally saw Eddie, he found nothing. Six weeks later, there were X rays. Still nothing. Yet Muskrat was uneasy; she insisted his health was deteriorating.

In June the gates opened, releasing the insanity of summer. Muskrat and Eddie left on a long trip through the West. I fed their stock while they were away, and was busy as usual with trespassers, maintenance, cutting wood for winter. I missed them, but I was glad for more time alone. I forgot about Eddie's problem. I had too many of my own.

One was that, with Muskrat's truck gone, I had no way to haul the firewood I cut in the forest. In addition, the old heap I'd been given as an act of "charity" was not only too expensive to run, it was also useless for the woods.

From a monastic point of view, it was false poverty to keep it. From the point of view of being poor, it was the classic catch-22 of pouring money down a rat hole or plunging deeply into debt.

Knowing nothing about pickups, I'd asked the opinion of Hunter people, most of whom bought American, some of whom swore by a particular import. I thought about buying a used truck, but, ignorant of auto repair, realized that this option, too, would only complicate my life. In the end, I made a maverick decision and bought what I needed: a king cab diesel, cheap to run, hard to find.

The same day I bought the truck, I saw a small motorbike on sale for the price of a set of tires—tires don't last long on Hunter roads. I shut my eyes, took a deep breath, and bought that, too, for scooting up to Muskrat's and over the ridge to the village.

I had never owned a vehicle before and was surprised and amused at the delight I took in my bright yellow pickup with racing stripes, or in strapping on my crash helmet and purring into the village on the bike. I had thought of these purchases in strictly utilitarian terms, but they became my pride and joy. I was gleeful as a child with her first trike.

A friend came to stay, allowing me to make a rare, quick visit to my aging parents, who lived in another state. My father was standing in the drive as I skidded in, showing off.

"What do you call that thing, the Yellow Peril?" he quipped, bemused at the sight of his daughter driving a form of transportation hitherto unknown in family history. The name stuck.

Back in the canyon, I contended with problems more difficult than trespassers and firewood. Busyness could divert my consciousness, but I was far from healed. It was the first time I had really been alone since I came to Hunter, and I was confronted with the need to sort out my thoughts, to confront the feelings that were still at war, even though I had begun to have some distance from the past.

Truths began to surface that I had not, probably could not have, absorbed, sustained, or faced earlier. There were painful insights about myself, about other people with whom I had been involved, about contemporary efforts to establish or reorganize communities. Underlying all was the constant tension between individual need for healthy solitude to make healthy community, and the corruption of the community ideal into lust for making people into abstract objects, forced to conform to an aesthetic ideal at the expense of their humanity.

This tension exists everywhere, not only in self-conscious communities. When people came to stay in the LSD castle, I invariably had to explain myself. They had been told only that a mysterious "solitary" was caretaker. Why wasn't I wearing a medieval habit? Why was I talking? Why wasn't I walled up? Why didn't I have green hair? I don't know where they thought the firewood might have come from, or who would clean the toilets, or keep the bikers out if I had sat on the porch in my white habit being decorative.

For self-conscious communities, though, nostalgia and romanticism had poisoned the new swill. Mythos denied historical realities, refused to look at old texts either on their own terms or with a critical eye. It blinded commonsense knowledge that neither the problems and dangers nor the supposedly novel proposals were original.

This denial, coupled with human hunger for control and power, leads to exactly the sort of thing I had run into time after time, and was running into again with the organization that owned the property in Hunter: devotion to expediency, no matter what the gospel ideal; the habit of whitewashing to maintain appearances, no matter how great the lie; insistence on "forgiveness" that meant return to sick reactive cycles of behavior.

But it was the trespassers and the violence of my reaction to them that forced me to come to terms with unpleasant realities in myself: my need for acceptance, which, in the end, amounted to seeking the very sort of status and power I had renounced; my vulnerability to those in control; my fear of insecurity and homelessness. The lessons of solitude were relentless, though I didn't really feel that I was learning anything, or that much had changed.

I can write these words now, but the questions they reflect, as I went about my summer chores and monastic routine, were anything but clear at the time. I confused my pain with what I perceived as an inability to forgive. I fought to arrive at what I thought was forgiveness, only to discover, as I pursued that chimera, that I was becoming more deeply entangled in the darkness that surrounded and penetrated me.

I tried every spiritual technique I had ever heard of, reaching for an artificial blankness of mind, the stereotype of "peace" I had been conditioned to seek. I began to understand that those who like to have strong women to lean on hate the creativity and truth that makes them strong, and are the most determined enforcers of this false peace.

Finally, gently, it was brought home that I was attempting a futile task, that true peace *is* engagement with darkness, a steady course that travels through its heart, through the flames of purification. When I was willing to stop trying to conform to a limited model, when I ceased trying to manipulate grace at work in the depths of my being, only then, by allowing this process to run its natural course, could I begin to understand the nature of true peace. All I could contribute to the effort was willingness: willingness to be done to, to be seared, to let go precious anger and resentment that gave me the illusion of control over the process of forgiveness.

I began to understand the wise monk's simple word: "In the struggle to forgive you are forgiving, and healing the others, too, even though there may be no awareness."

I began to move away from the static and somewhat accusatory language of "true self" and "false self." Instead I saw that, like galaxies born of elements swirling in the cosmic plasma, my self was fluid, lovingly created in every moment—if only I would trust, and allow it to come to be.

As with the galaxies, every element was needed, both

what I regarded as "good" and what I was ashamed of as "bad." These were human judgments. I could not see from the perspective of the Creator, who discards nothing, who in every moment infuses the self with the divine, newly responsive to the rest of creation as it is freshly brought to being. I had to stop trying to wrench my self in one direction or another; I had to have faith that my willingness was cocreating the unseen pattern with the Patterner, that nothing would be wasted.

All of these currents swirled through the activities of solitary prayer by day and by night: walking dogs; cutting wood; gardening; buying groceries; cleaning the castle for the few visitors; zipping up to Muskrat's on the 50cc motorcycle, or to the village to get our mail; wandering through the enchanted forest or in still-prayer; staring into the fire after the Evening Office, or Vigils in the small hours of the morning.

Sometimes they seemed to gather in a vortex that threatened to overwhelm me. In these moments, I understood that to do anything but remain willing in the stillness would be an abuse of the creation, a consent to hubris that said I knew better than God.

I went to the river's mouth when I needed reassurance. The sea, too, was God's gift. Beyond the rough water . . . on the other side was more darkness, yes, but having a different quality. On the other side was the knowledge that comes with *willingness not to know,* to ungrasp, the knowledge of mercy beyond sensibility.

Whenever I was pressed hard, Muskrat's stocky figure seemed to appear in my mind's eye, as if she had the gift of multiple presence. She was dressed in her usual costume of jeans, decrepit running shoes, baggy sweatshirt, and battered green hunting vest. Her jugular gaze pierced me from behind her clear-rimmed specs; her face was encircled by short, tightly curled gray hair.

In these moments of maelstrom that called forth her ghostly guardian presence, everything seemed to resolve into one principle: not what had happened or what had been done, but what mercy would make of it. The choice was mine, as it had been and continued to be hers.

Indian summer lay on us, an unusually dry one, when Muskrat and Eddie finally returned. The rains were late, and fire tension once again crackled through the tinder-dry mountains.

In the midst of this autumn there was one blessing: the gates were closed. The cats had come up the creek to remove the crossing. It wouldn't wash out this year.

The gravel was neatly piled on either bank until next spring, when the monstrous D-niner and the smaller D-six moved it again. The two snarling tracklayers would do-si-do up and down the creekbanks, pushing and sculpting, laying the big culvert on its stony bed, covering it to make a temporary road. It was a half-day job that called for muffins and hot coffee at midmorning.

Rosinda

I was up at Muskrat's place feeding stock when, late one afternoon, she and Eddie drove in.

Two things immediately were apparent.

Eddie was truly ill with some wasting sickness.

But lousy as he felt, his interest was focused elsewhere. For once I had driven my truck up the ridge instead of riding the motorbike, and he couldn't take his eyes off it. Unlike other Hunter denizens, more bound by convention, he was green with envy, entranced with the logical efficiency of the Yellow Peril's design.

To make matters worse, he had found and bought a second-hand pickup in Colorado, and had persuaded a friend to drive it back. Eddie was now too weak to do much driving. But he sure liked my truck.

I left after a few minutes' tale-telling. Both Muskrat and Eddie were very tired.

Exhaustion and worry shadowed Muskrat's face when she first came alone to see me.

"Them doctors are so sure of theirselves, an' they don't know from shit. I know they're missin' somethin'; they're too busy an' they don't give a damn."

After seeing Eddie, I had to agree.

"So make a fuss. Make them care. Make them understand there's something serious. Have you got another appointment?"

"Yeah, but I'm afraid it'll be the same old thing. An' it isn't just him bein' weak an' short of breath. He's actin' more and more funny. I can't rightly put my finger on it to describe exactly what's different, but he isn't himself. What's more, he falls down now an' again."

More X rays were taken. Muskrat and Eddie were called in for the results. Muskrat was nearly beside herself before they left for town that day. She would phone me when they got back.

The afternoon wore on. I put down my shuttle and covered the loom threaded with a pliant, glowing warp of garnet, umber, rust. Suddenly this work I loved seemed irrelevant, almost trivial.

I sat on the porch through the afternoon heat until dusk, the dogs snoozing at my feet. Little birds bathed in the margins of the creek; kingfishers rattled upstream and down, defending their territories; butterflies lazed over the bright mosaic of zinnias and dahlias in my garden; a pair of normally secretive wood ducks frolicked in the slow current, unaware of observing eyes, or familiar enough by now not to care. A nursery of eighteen young mergansers and their guardians swam by, darting after minnows under water, fighting mock battles, making enough racket to set the dogs barking.

"Well done!" I yelled after them. It took some doing to raise young in that forest of predators that slithered, climbed, and swooped.

Dusk was bleeding into darkness when I could wait no longer. I was just getting to my feet . . .

The phone rang.

Sobs reached me even before I put the receiver to my ear.

Muskrat, who'd had the tears beat out of her, was weeping.

"I'b sorry . . ."

"Muskrat! Take it easy . . ."

"It's Eddie . . . goddam doctors . . . missed the shadow. In his lung . . . an' now . . . now . . ."

I said the awful word for her.

"Metastasized?"

"Yeah. . . . Tomorrow . . . tomorrow we have to go to the city center to see a specialist who wants to take some tissue from his lung an' will confirm . . ."

More sobbing.

"Do you want me to come up?"

"No, not tonight. We're so tired; we're just gonna go to bed. . . . But . . . this is a lot to ask. . . . Could you come with us tomorrow? Eddie's never been to a hospital in his life, an' he's scared. He wants you to come along."

"Sure. . . ."

"Wear your habit will you?"

"Yes."

"I can't believe this is happening. We'll pick you up at nine."

I thought of Eddie's robust good health, his knotted arms pulling on the water pipe, the strength with which he tossed rounds of firewood like Frisbees into the back of his truck.

Why the habit? Eddie was Catholic, but hadn't been near a church in decades. He knew I was Anglican, or maybe didn't care.

Better not think about it. Better get some sleep.

Muskrat had never seen the procedure (a bronchoscopy) done, and Eddie'd never heard of it. After the clumsy, delayed diagnosis, they weren't trusting anyone medical. I'd had a bronchoscopy in college, and explained, as gently as I could, what probably would be done, how, barring narrow, twisted bronchial tubes (such as I have), it wouldn't hurt, especially if he could consciously relax. They would drip anesthetic down the back of his throat, and he might feel sick for a few minutes, but there was no shame in urping. It would be over quickly, and he'd be none the worse for wear.

It seemed to help to have a blow-by-blow description ahead of time. Like the mechanic he was, Eddie felt things should be done methodically. Nasty surprises weren't welcome. All the more reason he resented the botched X-ray readings.

He wasn't fooled; neither was Muskrat. We knew what we'd hear, yet somehow belief wouldn't come until the dread words were pronounced.

We arrived at the large teaching hospital and were directed to the fourth floor, where we met the specialist, whom we all liked, thank goodness.

Eddie was led away.

Muskrat and I thumbed through old magazines, insulted each other, then just sat there, holding hands. It seemed to take a very long time. Finally a nurse appeared, and we followed her to the small examination room.

Eddie was sitting on the edge of the table, bent over, fumbling for the buttons on his blue cowboy shirt.

"How'd it go, honey?"

Muskrat wanted to help him, but realized she'd embarrass him in front of the doctor if she did.

The doctor was facing away from us toward the window, backlit by the bright day he was using to make a note on Eddie's chart. He turned when he heard Muskrat's voice.

Flecks dotted the front of his white coat. He seemed to loom above us; he spoke before Eddie could respond.

"It went very well. He was most cooperative."

His interruption made Eddie a small boy, and told us the verdict. As a condemned man, Eddie was no longer of interest. Distance had to be kept from dying patients to preserve clinical objectivity. . . .

"Fine . . . fine . . . not nearly so bad as I thought . . ." mumbled Eddie, trying to recover the dignity one thoughtless sentence had taken from him.

"We were able to get what we went in for," the doctor went on. The warmth that made us like him was replaced by the clinical lecture-room approach, "and it was what we expected. He . . ."

No! Not "he." Eddie's not a dead body yet, but a living, breathing, frightened human being. . . . Talk to him!

Muskrat stirred and turned away from the doctor toward Eddie. The doctor refused to take the hint.

"He has . . ." The medical term fell into the vacuum created by his dehumanizing approach. ". . . surgical intervention would accomplish nothing. . . . Radiation will help reduce the brain lesion so that he won't have these small seizures and fall. . . ."

The disembodied voice droned on.

Eddie was trying to digest the unfamiliar words. When the medical jargon trailed off, I tried to reorient the conversation to practical matters Eddie could understand, that would redirect the conversation to him.

"Yeah, Eddie, you hear that? You're supposed to stay off the roof."

Eddie ducked his head and laughed; Muskrat snorted. The doctor finally spoke to Eddie directly.

"Until the lesion is reduced, it is inadvisable . . ." but there was compassion in his face for the first time.

Questions began to tumble from Muskrat about the duration of treatment, side effects, protocols. Encouraged by familiar professional questions, the doctor once again detached himself from the man sitting on the edge of the table.

I looked at Eddie, and Eddie looked at me, shaking his head like a bear swarmed by bees. He was scared, and I knew he was scared, but he pulled himself upright and broke into the hum of conversation.

"Doc, I wanna know how long I've got. Is it weeks or months?"

"Now Mr. Rocha . . ."

From his height, the white-coated oracle inclined toward Eddie as if to indicate such questions were bad form. "That is very difficult to know . . . some months . . . year or two . . ." The doctor slid over the worst possibility and offered the best.

Eddie again shook his head against the confusion of ambiguities in the doctor's words. He'd come up to the hard question like a man and been palmed off. Eddie could explode like Mount St. Helens if he felt you were humbugging, but the intimidating surroundings subdued him. The explosion came later.

Tell him, you bastard. Can't you see he really wants to know?
Eddie asked again.

Again the doctor dodged.

Muskrat was ending the interview, distracting Eddie by helping him down from the table, by holding his good corduroy jacket with the leather patches on the elbows. It was a hot day, but Eddie was always cold now.

The formality of shaking hands all around was grotesque. We gave each other primates' signs of nonaggression, as if these gestures would keep reality at bay just a little longer, as if we were agreeing on a conspiracy even as we sealed the covenant with Death. We grimaced like skulls in a charnel house.

"Feel free to call me if you have any questions," intoned the doctor as we went out the door.

It was going to happen fast. I knew it in my bones. I wondered if Muskrat knew.

Muskrat and Eddie were already walking to the elevator. I trailed in their wake, absently memorizing names, offices. We went down in silence, and as we left the building, the list grew: entrance to hospital; entrance to emergency room. . . . Eddie would inevitably end up here when we could no longer care for him at home.

We got in the car. Muskrat wanted to drive, so I sat in back, trying to be invisible so that she and Eddie could get used to their new relationship. In the Latin tradition, Eddie had always insisted on appearing dominant. Now, in a few moments, not only his dominance but his life had been suspended. Muskrat had always been independent, but she let Eddie think he ran the roost until it rankled, and then she went ahead and did what she pleased without saying anything.

Especially now, she wanted Eddie to live as normally as possible, and I knew she was ready to keep the truth from him until she thought he could bear it, if he ever could. She was so busy trying to protect him—and herself—that she couldn't see that he needed and wanted to know, that he was ready to know. And I wasn't too sure she had come to the reality of the situation herself, even though we all knew, deep down.

Eddie wasn't articulate about his feelings. He was as extroverted as they come. But the times we'd gossiped about this or that person's health problems, or some new medical advance, he'd often said that, for all his love of things mechanical, he wanted no part of medical life-support machines if he should be taken "real sick."

From the back seat of the car, I watched his desire to know conflict with his desire not to know; his desperate grasping for a magic straw that would cure him, and his growing awareness that for death there is no cure. I followed the involuntary play of nerves across his shoulder blades and neck as first one, and then the other, won out.

"What about this radiation business," he grumbled.

"It's up to you, honey. We can find out about it an' then decide. Let's go home an' eat."

None of us had any breakfast. Eddie couldn't, and neither Muskrat nor I felt like it.

A worm began to gnaw at my vitals, but it was in the wrong place for hunger. I put my hands under my scapular and held my belly, remembering the Spartan boy who concealed the fox.

As the words crawled back and forth in the front seat, I memorized street names, freeway exits, mileage, until we came to the familiar turnoff. Muskrat drove steadily and well, and soon we were lurching and bumping up the scarp, a rooster tail of dust trailing behind us. We came to the triple fork in the road, and I jumped out to open Muskrat's gate.

We drove the half mile through the woods onto the open ridge crest, dipped down, then up, and pulled under the carport by the mobile. All four of Muskrat's dogs jumped at the end of their chains, trying to reach their beloved master and mistress. Neither Muskrat nor Eddie seemed to notice as we went inside.

Muskrat set herself to make breakfast, having waved me over to sit with Eddie at the table in front of the picture window. Eddie, surrounded by comforting presences, was like a man waking out of a nightmare only to find that the monster he faced with his eyes open was far more terrifying than the monster haunting his dreams.

I had never before been in Eddie's house in my habit, and it made me uncomfortable. I pulled off my veil and made some business of folding it.

"That's better," said Eddie, "strip for action."

I made a face.

"It doesn't feel right to wear it around you all. . . . It's the great separator. At this point, I don't want to be separated."

Muskrat plonked coffee in front of us. She had sausage frying, and began beating eggs with a whisk in a yellow plastic bowl.

Eddie didn't say anything for a few minutes, but the pressure got too much for him, and his fierce desire for the truth overcame all his fear.

"Damn!" His fist hit the table, slopping our mugs. "I always wanted it to come quick! How come this dyin' business takes so damn long?"

He was ready. Muskrat was not.

With a silent apology for what I feared was betrayal, yet knowing that Eddie wanted the real options, I met his eyes and said gently, "This kind can be quick—it largely depends on what you really want, what you most deeply want. . . ."

His face registered shock, relief, gratitude in fleeting succession, before fear returned, and confusion.

I hurried on to repeat the doctor's words, ". . . but of course there's no telling for sure; there are so many factors. A lot of people have beat the odds. . . ."

Eddie picked up on this as Muskrat put plates of breakfast on the dark green plastic mats in front of us, and crumpled into a chair.

"You hear that, honey?" There was false heartiness in his voice as he tried bravely to cheer us all. "You hear that? We got twenty years."

We picked up his cue and ate our breakfast with some semblance of normality. At least we were there together; at least the coffee was strong, the eggs full of herbs and cheese, the hot sweet rolls melting on the tongue.

It wasn't that we were fooling ourselves; rather that emotional absorption progressed in each of us at different rates, and we wanted to live to the full what life was left.

━━━

It was our last meal together. Muskrat said it was the last time Eddie ever wanted to talk about being sick, or spoke honestly about his death. He had the answer he wanted.

"But you was right to tell him," she said later, when she was able to snatch time for a brief visit at the cabin one sallow muggy afternoon. "It's just that . . ."

She sat in the rice-straw chair with the bookcase behind her back. Kelly slept across her feet, Pomo on mine. Under the freckles, her milky skin had become pasty from exhaustion and strain. "But he had to know. An' I was thinkin', how'm I gonna tell him. An' then you said it. But now, of course, you're Death for him. You're Truth."

"What do you mean?"

"Well, like every once in a while somethin' will break, or the generators need cleanin', an' he'll say, get Maggie, an' then a minute later he'll say, no, don't get Maggie, get someone else. He wants to see you but he don't."

"That's not surprising. Don't feel like you have to make me feel good about it. Have you kept up the radiation?"

I went with them the first time. I waited in the car. When they came out, Eddie started babbling with relief. "It's nuthin'," he said, with the disbelief of one who has looked into the executioner's face only to find he has been reprieved. "We got twenty years, honey." This had become his refrain, his incantation against the dark.

O God, don't let him have a reaction. . . .

"Yeah, seems like the only thing to do. I don't like it, but he's had some bad falls. I dunno if he's graspin' at straws or if he's doin' it because he thinks I want him to. Anyway, I dunno how I really feel. I'm numb. We went to look at his new truck."

"His *what?*"

"Oh, he's got this idea he wants a fancy truck. We went an' looked at several, an' his idea just gets bigger an' bigger. He wants one o' them big crew cab outfits, with dual rear wheels an' a humongous diesel engine—6.2, I think, with every extra. . . . What are you laughin' at?"

I was beside myself, tears pouring down my cheeks, clutching my belly in which some demon grasped a piece of sinew between hot pincers and twisted.

"It's the Yellow Peril."

"It's the *what?*"

"My pickup. You know, my father named it the Yellow Peril."

"Yeah, I know, but what does that have to do with Eddie?"

"He's jealous, that's what. He's exerting control over the rest of his life by buying a truck that not only equals mine, but is so far out I'll never be able to catch him. What's more," I doubled up again, half with giggles, half in agony, "if I am Death to him, this is his way of beating Death. Isn't that just like him! But if it makes him feel better, why not? Only, what are you going to do with it? Can you drive it?"

"Not very well. If he really does decide to get it, it'll be on fleet order, so it'll take awhile. I think it's a cuckoo idea. I'd sell it, maybe. . . . Oh shit, I can't think about that yet."

"Do you have time to go to the coast? You look like you need to get away."

"No. Rod's only going to be up at our place an hour or so. I can't leave Eddie alone. He gets a little funny, an' the medication makes him foggy. I have to get back."

"Just remember, I'm on call twenty-four hours a day."

"Yeah," said Muskrat, sitting there without moving, "thanks."

We continued to sit, looking at our fingers in our laps. Muskrat lifted her head and summed it all up.

"Shit," she said deliberately, "shit."

A soft sound made us look out the window.

It was raining.

Deathwatch

It was raining.

I sat in front of the fire in the pitch black January night, wondering when the next blow would fall. The flames spoke to spirits in the redwood walls that flickered their silent reply.

Pomo lay in her nest on the hearth. When she got too warm, she would loll back, hanging halfway out over the edge of the yellow firebrick, her head on Kelly's bed, and begin gently to snore. Kelly, with his long hair, was always too hot on evenings when I sat and stared into the fire. He had gone to sleep behind my chair.

The rain whispered outside, an occasional metallic *plock!* striking the stovepipe, when water accumulated in a large drop on the end of a branch, and fell. The creek was up but not in flood: its endless muttering was at first soothing, then an added irritant to my growing restlessness. . . .

All this Sunday evening coziness and comfort conflicted with Muskrat's and Eddie's painful progress through the last weeks of his life. He was going fast, but because we could see the day-by-day deterioration, the unvoiced agony, it seemed interminable.

It was as if we had known no other life, as if the solemn, dull, painful drip of winter was eternal, as if the sun and the sea had never existed, nor laughter, nor joy. Whenever Muskrat could find someone to stay with him for an hour or so, which was becoming increasingly difficult as his mental state deteriorated, she'd come down. Aside from buying groceries for both of us, I stayed home in case she did.

A few weeks after the radiation treatments began, her car barreled down the hill through the gate. She was shaking as she got out, and almost ran up the steps into the cabin. I grabbed her, sat her in a chair, gave her a cup of herb tea.

"It don't seem right that we keep *screamin'* at each other!"

Muskrat was as close to frantic as I'd ever seen her.

"Each time I swear I won't respond in kind, an' each time he screams my nerves snap an' I scream back."

"Maybe it's just as well."

"It don't *feel* well."

"Yeah, but when Eddie pushes your buttons it's sort of like the truck, something tangible, something he can trigger and manipulate that will give a predictable response, unlike his sickness, which is out of control. Your reaction is dependable—even if it isn't pleasant."

"I hadn't thought of that."

"You can't think of everything, and you have to stop trying to do it all yourself. Medical people aren't supposed to treat their own families, remember?"

"Yeah, but . . ."

The worst time had been a week earlier when she told me about the effects of the radiation. She was in tears.

"It isn't that he's losin' his hair—though that's been real hard on his vanity. They're *burnin'* him! He's just burnt to a crisp. I keep tellin' 'em, for God sake, *look* at him, but the technician says he don't need to see the doctor and just shoves him in the room an' gives him more an' more. He's blisterin' somethin' awful, an' he's got thrush so bad in his mouth an' throat he can't eat. He's so damn skinny already."

"What about the local internist?"

"I tried to get an appointment."

"Sounds like an emergency to me. What about the X rays?"

"At least the lesion's reduced; he isn't fallin' like he was, but he can't do nothin', either, an' his brains is gettin' scrambled."

Then for the first time,

"I just dunno how much longer I can go on."

At Christmas she had taken him to the hospital with pneumonia.

I could have kicked myself for being away, but for more than a year I'd promised my family I'd spend Christmas with them. Muskrat insisted I go, and so I was hundreds of miles away when it happened. I finally reached her by phone. She was almost incoherent.

"Just got him back from the hospital. He sure hates hospitals. He never stayed in one in his whole life. Now Lizzie's lookin' to die—I mean, she would have to go an' do that when he can hardly travel."

Lizzie was Eddie's ninety-two-year-old mother.

Lizzie did die while I was away. Though Muskrat didn't say much about the funeral, she was haggard when I returned.

"All I can say is I doubt that family'll go near the Catholic church again. He was a real arrogant in-a-hurry sonofabitch."

I thought of the perfunctory, twenty-minute, rush-in, rush-out Mass at the village Catholic church. I'd gone once. A bored, banal, barroom-piano-playing celebrant who took no trouble to hide his contempt for country people in a homily that would have insulted five-year-olds. But Muskrat's voice was tottering on. . . .

"An' to top it off, I found out I'm the executor of Lizzie's estate, an' I got all them vultures around."

"At least it gives you something else to think about."

"I don't need nothin' more to think about."

"How is he?"

"Weak, but now we got him off the damn radiation he's doin' better. I got the thrush mostly cleared from his throat, an' while he can't eat good, at least he isn't hurtin' so bad. The doctor at the hospital nearly had a fit when he saw him. He asked me, why didn't I tell the radiologist he was burnin' so bad, an' I kept sayin', I *did*, but they wouldn't *lissen*. . . ."

She was weeping now. Years after Eddie died, she still hasn't come to terms with the callousness of the people in the radiology office.

"Have you ever been back?" I will ask, when the subject comes up. "They really need to know how you feel, and you need to tell them."

"I just don't trust myself," she'll reply. "I just don't know what I'd do if I tried to tell 'em. I dunno if I'd break down, or if I'd go for 'em."

≈

The fire sighed and sputtered. A log burned through and fell.

I wondered if I had enough energy to put on another, wait for it to catch, bank it, climb the ladder to bed. But something more than lethargy held me in my chair: I was waiting for the phone to ring.

By now Muskrat and Eddie had drawn a cocoon around themselves. Eddie became restive if she was out of his sight or hearing, and she didn't want to leave him. It wouldn't be long. . . .

Muskrat still phoned me every morning, but our conversations were perfunctory. No banter. No change in Eddie. Lists of things needed, groceries. We'd meet at the top of the ridge, shift brown paper bags from the Yellow Peril to her Subaru, and stand silently in the damp, staring down at spirals of smoke rising from village stovepipes.

"Don't seem like we're still in the world," she'd said three days ago on a cold, bright morning, as we watched a heavily pregnant doe creeping through the scrub below us along the rim of the scarp. "I know the world's there an' goes on, but somehow Eddie an' me aren't in it."

"How is he?"

"'Bout the same. I think he's gettin' weaker, but like it's been all along, not somethin' I can exactly put my finger on. It don't seem like any amount of heat'll keep him warm, an' I get worried 'cause sometimes he'll take a notion to prowl around when I'm not lookin'. He's startin' to hide things. An' . . ."

"And what?"

"I keep hearin' Lizzie *callin'* him. I think he hears her, too. He was her baby, an' I can't imagine her ever lettin' go of him. It makes me mad."

Muskrat's words gave me the cold creeps. She had mother-in-law problems even in death.

It wasn't just the intuitive knowledge you sometimes get when you know you're saying good-bye to someone for the last time, and there is joy in the sorrow of letting go, of loss gladly, if painfully, received. It was rather Lizzie's *not* being able to let go, and Eddie's *not* being able to be free about his own dying.

And Muskrat was too close, too close to see she hadn't the objectivity she thought she did, too caught in the tussle over him with Lizzie on the other side of the curtain, all of which fed her denial. Denial that was just as well, because it protected her as the agony stretched out for days, and the weeks followed one on another.

I shivered.

The fire was nearly out.

Kelly had crept around my feet and was curled in his nest. Pomo was wound in a tight ball in hers, nose buried under a back leg and her tail. Its tip wiggled as she caught my eye, encouraging me to add another log to the cooling embers.

When she first came to the cabin, she'd never seen a wood stove before, but it didn't take her long to figure it out. When the fire went out the first night I forgot to bank it, she came to the bottom of the loft ladder and woke me up. I thought she had to go out, but no, after I had come down and opened the door, she went over to the stove, put a paw on it, turned her head over her shoulder, and woofed. When her dumb mistress finally got the message, she dived in her nest and squirmed around, offering her tummy to be rubbed, more to reward me than as an act of submission.

Rosinda

I put a couple of logs on, opened the damper until they caught, closed it enough to keep the heat in but let the smoke out, and settled back in my chair.

Have to bring some more wood in tomorrow. . . .

It wasn't a happy prospect; I seemed always to be tired these days, and lifting the logs had triggered a little switchblade of pain in my belly.

My thoughts went back to Muskrat and Eddie. Talk about solitaries! I felt ashamed. . . . But as I considered the false distinction between a "monastic" solitude and the solitude of ordinary people, the questions that had crystallized the previous autumn began to resolve themselves.

Contact with people in Hunter had made me realize that solitude breaks down distinctions. All of us are solitaries: we are born alone through the birth canal into the world and time, and we die alone. No one can enter our interior experience, or its continuum with the outer world we call community.

Solitude is the human condition, the universal vocation to be human. It is the willingness, with Love indwelling, to go to the heart of pain to find new life and share it with the world even through you may be separated from it physically. It is from this commitment to be focused through the narrow gate of solitude that self-emptying love is out-poured, and the heart of the community, the heart of its pain, is transformed into the heart of joy.

I saw this commitment incarnated in Muskrat, though she would deny it. Day after day, little by little, I glimpsed her suffering and the choices she made consciously, deliberately; choices against bitterness, anger, resentment, revenge. Her motives were always mixed, but the clear flame of her integrity burned bright.

Often her choices arose from the damage she had suffered, but she knew this; sometimes, because she needed to define herself by giving. But she understood that self-giving and self-emptying are not the same, that the former can be a trap for giver and receiver alike, a power trip, a controlling ego. Whereas the latter . . . the latter went against all self-aggrandizing; even, sometimes, against common sense, at least when judged by the standards of the marketplace.

Her choices never became automatic. Often I witnessed her anguish as she was torn between revenge and reconciliation in the conflicts that inevitably arose from the petty politics of the village, and now with Eddie.

I don't know if she was conscious of what I saw. But the thrust was always the same: to neutralize the evil and pain that she had received; to render them impotent and transform them wherever she found them; to heal whenever the opportunity arose, not by the illusory imposed power of self-mastery, moral imperatives, or manipulation, but by realizing grace present in and through her own and other's helplessness, by acknowledging and working within real material and physical limitations. She never spoke in religious terms; she rarely mentioned God; her piety was her living.

She showed me that solitude is complete reliance on self-emptying Mercy, that solitude is always a stranger and sojourner, homeless, a bag lady.

The insights poured out in a relentless flood.

Solitude precludes the empire building that attaches to property, physical or mental (yours or someone else's); solitude rules out security and physical stability that rely on legal agreements, which, if you're poor, will invariably lead to exploitation.

Solitude is disengagement from human power struggles in order to have the detachment and clear-sightedness to undertake true political action with integrity. Solitude is living simply and, for the likes of me, singly, through doing for yourself as opposed to having an elaborate network of people to support an artificial enclosure and an artificial image.

Solitude seeks the humility of vulnerability, available to the Muskrats of this world and taught by them, the desert saints of our age in anything but traditional guise. Solitude is the willingness to penetrate illusion at any price, especially the illusion supported by religious aesthetes who would perpetuate form at the expense of transfiguration.

If beauty is locked into the booths of static criteria it becomes self-conscious; it no longer is beauty. It is dead. If we lose beauty, we have nowhere to take our pain. And solitude is willingness to be taken to levels of pain that are universal, to the abyss of despair where alone the fullness of Mercy is able to enter our emptied-out selves.

Solitude is facing through self-deception, admitting the capacity for evil that only you can choose, just as the good you may contribute is unique. Choose to pay the price, or retreat into control and closed systems that intensify slavery to real or imagined fear.

Solitude is admitting ugly words: rape, rapist, victim. Rape is psychological and spiritual, the violation of a relationship of trust that is intangible, elusive, as damaging as the physical act, which is never confined to the body alone.

Solitude is solidarity with raped, powerless, and exploited people everywhere, knowing in yourself the guilt of the rapist, the horror of the raped, understanding that in the end there are no boundaries, no convenient encapsulations, whatever form rape takes—physical, spiritual, economic. Disorientation, disinformation, devaluation of individuals or entire peoples create the rage and violence of this world.

But if you are a cause of stumbling to one of these little ones who have faith, it would be better for you to have a millstone hung round your neck and be drowned in the depths of the sea. Alas for the world that such causes of stumbling arise! Come they must, but woe betide those through whom they come!

Solitude is admitting the humiliation that, like other women, professionally trained in discernment, well educated, categorized by others (not always as a compliment) as "strong," I am just as subject to the culturally inculcated paralysis that immobilizes us in the face of aggression, to the artificial blankness of mind that makes us prey to physical force or slander, the menace that is the subtext of an insistent male's anger. Like other poor people, I am just as vulnerable to terrorism by members of hierarchies who are immersed in the denial that covers up what they do not want to see and are afraid to know, who destroy by turning truth on its head, so that the victim becomes the criminal.

On the other hand, solitude is also facing the fact that I have in some degree cooperated in becoming a victim, no matter what the extenuating circumstances.

Solitude is admitting the mixture of emotions and fears that led to my having stayed in damaging environments as long as I did, and which exist in any human situation. This admission precludes simplistic black-and-white judgments about guilt and vindication. Solitude unlocks compassion for impossible situations in which the fear and pain of human existence cannot be sorted into simple categories of guilt and blame. Each of us hurts others merely by existing; life feeds upon life.

Solitude is willingness to face these complexities, to be cauterized to the depths of the soul's infection so that healing may occur, a healing that does not cover running sores, but transfigures them in the wounds of a God willingly ruined for the sake of creation.

～～～

A thump and flying sparks broke my reverie. The two logs I had put on the fire—how long ago? what time could it possibly be?—had burned through. I hauled myself carefully out of the chair, not wanting to reawaken the nasty creature in my middle, replenished the fire, sat down again.

The dogs snored on.

But the worm in my gut wasn't asleep. It took another bite as it always seemed to now whenever I exerted myself. I chalked it up to stress, waited for the spasm to pass, for reverie to return. But my mood was broken.

The embers glowed, but they were alien and cold.

And now that I am old and gray-headed, O God, do not forsake me. . . .

What nonsense! I shook myself from self-dramatization. I was only forty-three. I welcome my gray hairs. I earn them.

But, as so often happens, the psalm was for someone else.

You have showed me great troubles and adversities, but you will restore my life and bring me up again from the deep places of the earth.

You strengthen me more and more; you enfold and comfort me. Therefore I will praise you. . . .

I removed the wire fire screen, banked the coals, adjusted the damper, closed the stove doors. Too weary to fix myself a hot water bottle, I climbed into my icy bed in the loft, and curled up inside my flannel nightgown, shutting out cold, sorrow, and the ache in my belly.

～～～

The phone started ringing.

For a moment I wasn't sure where I was. Then I nearly fell off the ladder, bumbling down to grab it. Our conversation was abrupt.

"Can you come?"

"Be right up."

I let the dogs out while I dressed. They sensed something was wrong, and were back by the time I'd pulled on my clothes. I locked them in and walked out into the blackness under the rain-soaked firs to the shed. It was as if I had rehearsed this night, these steps, the cold unsentimental reality, the strange sense of competence in the face of whatever I would find up at Muskrat's.

I pulled out the choke; the diesel caught on the first try. I warmed the engine for a few moments, easing the choke until it ran without vibration, and backed out of the shed. The wheels caught the greasy mud as I accelerated slowly through the gate, got out, closed and locked it, continued up the muddy road through the sodden forest.

Lights were on at Muskrat's. I could see them as I drove along her road out of the woods into the open, before dropping down into the saddle and up again. She appeared, fully dressed, before I got out of the cab.

"We'll take mine. I'll drive. Can you help me get him in?"

Eddie may have been thin, but he was still heavy. Although he was drifting in and out of consciousness, he tried, unsuccessfully, to help us move him across the room and outside. He was annoyed by his weakness even as he lost touch with his surroundings.

He was almost a deadweight as we struggled to slide him into the car. He slumped in the seat too low to fasten the belt around him. I got in back, while Muskrat locked the house. Eddie's breathing rasped, and then I couldn't hear anything at all.

We started down the dark mountain. Muskrat drove gently, but Eddie's unsecured body kept sliding. I held him from the back as best I could. By the time we got to the bottom of the scarp and turned on the road through the sleeping village, I knew Eddie had to sit upright or he would die in the car.

"Can you stop? I think I can lift him from behind, if you'll help me."

Muskrat pulled over and we got him strapped in. Now he sagged forward against the shoulder strap. She started the car and pulled out on the rain-slicked road.

"I hope I'm doin' the right thing."

I was appalled.

"How is it *not* right?"

Muskrat had a rule about not talking frankly in front of a sick person, no matter how comatose, so I couldn't ask what I wanted to know: *how long has he been like this?*

"Well, it may be a false alarm, but his breathin' isn't right, and I thought maybe I better take him down. Sorry to drag you out."

"I thought I told you to stop apologizing."

I couldn't hear any breathing. I wondered if Eddie would last until we got to the hospital. I began to realize how Muskrat's long confinement with the sick man had narrowed her perception. Suffering had mesmerized and encapsulated her.

"Let me know if you want me to drive."

"I'm OK."

Her hands clutched the wheel, arthritic knuckles showing white and distended in the greenish light from the panel.

"You sure?"

"Yeah. I couldn't just sit."

We had turned onto the interstate before she spoke again. "How is he?"

"No change," I said, wondering if Eddie were still alive. There had been no sound or movement for many miles.

"I can't go any faster; the road's too wet, an' we'll start planin'."

"A few minutes one way or the other won't make any difference."

Suddenly I realized she might think I meant Eddie'd died. I felt his neck and found a feeble pulse. "He's OK."

Eddie stirred at my touch.

I snatched my hand away to avoid irritating him more.

He mumbled something I couldn't catch.

"You're in the car, honey. We're going to the hospital."

A feeble protest came from the sick man.

"Just for tonight, honey, just until you're breathin' right."

Eddie was still.

The freeway spread in front of us, six lanes of slippery blacktop broken by white fluorescent stripes. Except for a few eighteen-wheelers whining past, there was no one else on the road.

"You go in," said Muskrat, "an' tell 'em we need a gurney. Tell 'em . . ." Her voice broke.

"All right. If there's a crowd, I'll use my elbows."

We drove to the emergency entrance.

"Wait'll I stop," Muskrat complained from force of habit as I jumped out. I tried not to run as I burst through the metal door.

The place was empty.

For a moment I wondered if I were dreaming, if the dying man, the worried woman, the drive through the night and the rain were a surreal fantasy about to become a nightmare in a phantom hospital where I searched for help through a maze of corridors. . . .

The duty nurse emerged from an office.

"Can I help you?"

"We've got a very sick man outside. He can't come in under his own power. . . ."

The efficient medical routine was set in motion, at once sad and comforting. The nurse rang for an orderly. Together we managed Eddie into a wheelchair; it was easier than trying to lift him onto a gurney. I couldn't tell if he was breathing.

Muskrat went in to give the doctor his history.

Then we sat dazed and mute in the hard orange plastic chairs, while Eddie was taken away, stripped and examined somewhere out of our sight and control.

Muskrat looked gray in the harsh light. Her face was expressionless, her eyes sunken and dull. Then she roused herself, inclining sideways toward me.

"Well, we made it."

"Yeah. I wish you'd let me drive."

"He would've fussed."

"How long has he been like this?"

"A couple of days. I don't know why it took me so long to decide to bring him. I guess partly 'cause he hates hospitals an' machines so; partly 'cause we were so wrapped up in ourselves, partly . . ." she struggled for professional objectivity, ". . . partly 'cause I just can't seem to see things like I normally do. But then his breathin' got so bad, an' . . ."

"I'm glad you brought him, glad you phoned me. You've been nursing him too long alone. You've got to have a break. You've just got to."

She turned fully toward me as if seeing clearly for the first time.

"I wasn't sure he'd live until we got here."

A tight band burst from around my chest.

"I wondered if you knew."

"Part of me did. Part of me didn't. Part of me didn't want to. I hope I didn't hurt him by waitin' too long, but it would've been a hell of a fight gettin' him to come of his own free will."

"I have a feeling your timing is just about right. . . . Don't fret; you can't change anything now. . . ."

The orderly wheeled a gurney from the examination room, feet first.

I couldn't see whether the face of the body was covered. . . .

. . . but there was an I.V.

Eddie didn't move. He was asleep or unconscious.

The house physician pushed past the gurney. We rose from our seats.

"I've sedated him. He's got a fulminating pneumonia,

but he's not in trouble at the moment. We're admitting him."

We stood there like two dumb animals.

"There's nothing more for you to do until he wakes up," he said gently, taking Muskrat by the elbow and guiding her toward the door, "so I'd suggest you go home and get some sleep and come back in the morning."

Muskrat shook him off and pulled herself together. She went over to the gurney.

She kissed Eddie on the forehead between his closed eyes, saying clearly, "They're gonna keep you. You behave, hear? Maggie an' I'll be right back."

She became professional.

"What room's he goin' in? An' we can come back anytime?"

"Two–three–four. Yes, of course, you can come anytime."

"What about his family?"

She fixed him with her question.

"Why don't you wait until you come back to phone them?" came the coded reply.

She nodded.

We passed beyond the heavy door.

"I'm driving."

She handed me the keys.

The rain had stopped while we were inside, but it began again as I turned onto the freeway.

Tears.

The psalm surfaced in midphrase:

You have fed us with the bread of tears; you have given us bowls of tears to drink.

"I figure," said Muskrat, "we'll get a shower an' clothes an' come back. You're comin', aren't you?"

"You couldn't keep me away. How many days do you figure?"

"Two or three. What about the dogs? Jill will feed mine."

Jill was a member of the complex clan Muskrat had first married into. She lived about a mile north along the ridge.

"It should be late enough to phone when we get back. I'll call Shirley and ask her to stop by."

Shirley had just finished an accounting course and was studying at her parents' home for the CPA exam. She'd be glad of a chance to be alone for a bit.

The rain was coming harder now, large drops splattering on the windshield. I had to force myself to concentrate; my brain felt as if it had turned to sludge. I stayed in the slow lane.

"Weird, isn't it?"

Muskrat's question caught me just as I was dropping off at the wheel.

"What?"

"The whole thing. I feel like it's happenin' to someone else. I feel like somebody in a novel; maybe I been readin' too many novels. . . ."

Muskrat's appetite for novels was a local joke. Anything was grist for her mill, from serious literature to bodice rippers.

". . . I guess it's shock. I feel like I'm in some kind of TV drama, but I don't feel much except slightly split. I mean, everything I'm doin' an' sayin' is coming from my real place, but I still feel like I'm speakin' lines—an' watchin' the damn thing at the same time. I feel kinda guilty 'cause I'm so relieved. I oughta be grievin' for him, but I feel guilty 'cause I don't feel."

"You're exhausted, that's why."

"Yeah, I know, but still . . ."

"Cut it out, Superwoman."

"Shaddap."

"What time is it?"

Light was spilling across the valley from clouds piled silver along the mountains to the east.

"The Den will be open when we get to town. You want to stop? You really ought to eat something."

The Den was the local hangout for early risers: fisher-men, loggers, truckers. The food was basic eggs and bacon, and coffee flowed from a bottomless pot.

"You hungry?"

"Not really, but you ought to eat."

"You're a fine one to talk. What about my spare tire?"

"I hadn't noticed it lately. We can worry about spare tires when all this is over."

"Excuses, excuses."

I was awake now; the banter had eased the tension. The rain stopped; the road began to dry off.

I thought of the last time I'd made this trip with Muskrat, when we came back after the bronchoscopy. I'd been wearing my habit then, at Eddie's request. . . .

The habit reminded me of something else.

A few weeks ago, I'd gone to see the only Anglican vicar in the region. His church was in the town near the vineyard I used to manage. I'd driven over through the pruned vineyards, through barren vines, standing wet and stump-like. Few sights are more melancholy under a black and weeping sky.

I'd been wondering what to do if Eddie or someone in his family suddenly reverted to their childhood Catholicism, as Eddie had done that day when we went to see the specialist. I had some idea what might happen, but I wanted as much practical information as I could get, especially since the family seemed so alienated from religion. It was a delicate situation.

The vicar was one of those people who like solitaries in habits, decorative, meek. He was one of the last high-church clergy to sport a biretta, long after most of his Roman Catholic colleagues had given them up.

For all I know, he still wears one.

He put a cassock on at the slightest excuse, and when his daughters got too interested, he refused to let them serve at the altar any longer, something they'd done since they could walk.

He let women into the sanctuary—to clean it—only because there was no way to avoid it. He seemed to feel there was something unclean about having women too near the altar, as if they would defile it. For that matter, he seemed uncomfortable if *anyone* not in orders, male or female, got too close.

Nonetheless, we'd been friends for a long time. He'd helped me through the transition to solitude, though I suspect he was disappointed when I didn't turn out as he'd hoped.

As I drove into town, I braced myself for what he'd say when he saw my pickup. He drove an ostentatiously battered truck (which he knew how to fix), one so old that it was showing off just to own it.

He kept it going on the excuse that he hauled food to Hispanic workers, most of whom were illegals. It was, he thought, his badge of solidarity with the poor. He had been made an honorary canon for his ministry, but nobody was fooled. With amused irony, the migrants nicknamed him *Padrecito.*

I parked in front of the church. He must have heard me coming, because the door of his office opened, and he poked his head out, a blue heron about to strike.

"Good heavens," he exclaimed, "is that the latest transportation for poverty-stricken hermits?"

I felt my hackles rise. My reasoning and my financing were none of his business. I wasn't in the mood to talk about anything but Eddie's dying.

We sat down with teacups, and I outlined the situation. I told him how Eddie asked me to wear my habit, how the family reacted after Lizzie's funeral. I watched his face set hard when he saw what was coming.

"So what do I do if he wants last rites, or his relatives insist? I haven't done much of this sort of thing. Can you give me some practical tips?"

"Get him a priest."

"He won't have one."

"Make him get a priest," the vicar insisted. "Priests administer rites. *Lay* people—and *you*," stabbing an ivory finger at me, "are a *lay* person—are ministered *to*."

In the months Eddie had been dying, Muskrat told me, he hadn't said much about religion. "He hates the Church like poison, and after goin' to Lizzie's funeral, I can see why. He always said you were his priest."

To be Eddie's priest was an honor and a responsibility, which was why I'd come. But I could see I was wasting my time. Wearily I tried to explain.

The vicar jumped to his feet.

The bony digit leapt closer and shook in my face.

"Well, you're *not* his priest, not by any stretch of the imagination, and wouldn't be even if you'd been through an ordination rite. Remember, you're a *woman*. Now go home and say your prayers and plan on getting him an RC priest."

"But what . . ."

"Stop wasting my time."

He retreated to the bridge of his nose.

He went to the door and held it open.

I wondered if he thought I'd come there just to annoy him.

I wondered if he was right.

Heavy with inadequacy, I drove back to Hunter.

It wasn't the first time this problem had come up. Groups coming to the LSD castle repeatedly asked me to preside at their worship, preach the word, heal the sick, lead them in the Breaking of Bread.

But I could not. We'd pray the liturgy up to the consecration—and then I'd have to pull out the Magic Cookies. The rector had reserved the Sacrament in my cabin for just such occasions.

People objected to this, but in those days things hadn't moved as far as they have now. To abort the liturgy like that was a travesty of our priesthood and the Eucharist, of worship, of indwelling love, of the knowledge that our lives are broken as Body and Blood.

How could outsiders in round collars presume to offer our pain in the breaking of bread? What did they know of our suffering? How could they see the beauty that transfigured our squalor? What did they know of poverty, of the struggle to survive? What did they know of the receiving end of exploitation? What could my vicar friend understand of Muskrat's life, even if he could summon the humility to try?

You are our priest.

I said no then. I would not say that now, nor would I hesitate. . . .

Clergy and bishops jealous of their arrogated power—nonordained people, concerned with getting the magic right—both groups shut out their own real problems. They are oblivious to people on the margins, who have no means of escaping their pain.

Hunter is too poor and too isolated for institutional churches to bother with. There is no money or prestige in it, no one to observe and reward a professional's good works with professional honors.

The question is, whether these clergy, and large numbers of convention-bound, nonordained folk, prefer marginalized humanity to go through their living and dying without sacraments, rather than risk breaking a rigid paternalistic code, a closed magic circle, by letting otherwise qualified people celebrate and administer them when appropriate. We should be taught this discernment before we are baptized; entrusted to exercise intelligence and self-restraint when we receive the rite. . . .

By the time we'd driven into town, the old rage was gnawing at me; my hands on the steering wheel had clenched into fists. I backed into a parking place in front of the Den.

We were hunched over mugs of steaming coffee, waiting for our eggs, when the cockatrice hatched in my womb.

A lake of pain rolled over my body. Across the bleared knotty pine tabletop set with maps of the river and local fishing holes, I vaguely glimpsed Muskrat, aghast. For a moment the paper river ran with real water, and a steelhead jumped in one of the pools.

"What is it? Your time?"

I couldn't look at her.

"No."

I tried to sound normal, but my throat was too tight. "Stress."

The word was a hiss.

"You seen your nice Jewish doctor lately?"

I shook my head.

"Well, your nice Jewish mother says you better get off your butt an' go see him."

Muskrat had a habit of raiding her motley ancestry for whatever avatar seemed appropriate to the moment.

I stuck out my tongue to distract her.

The waitress slapped our platters of eggs, bacon, muffins, hash browns, and pancakes in front of us.

"Everything OK here?"

The question was standard, but she didn't mean our breakfasts.

"Yeah, we're OK." I tried for an ordinary smile. "Thanks."

After she left, I glared at Muskrat with all the ferocity I could muster. "I'll see my nice Jewish doctor when all this is over with."

"Seems to me like you been havin' one cold after another this winter, an' . . ."

"Have you looked in the mirror lately?"

"You should talk."

"You're breakfast's getting cold. Eat."

Muskrat was hungry, and obediently began her meal. I pushed and poked at the puddle of yellow eggs, and finally choked down a blueberry muffin. Both of us hate waste, and I was ashamed to leave the uneaten meal congealing on the table.

"It doesn't matter," said Muskrat, absolving me, "let's get out of here."

We paid the cashier and continued toward Hunter. Muskrat drove.

Two hours later we were on the road again, having bathed, packed, made arrangements for our animals. We had brought a thermos and drank coffee as the Yellow Peril rolled along. The rain held off; the interstate was dry.

Muskrat let me drive after looking me up and down as if she thought I were trying to hide something under my white tunic, brown scapular, and black veil. She'd asked me to wear the habit; she also wanted to keep an eye on me.

"You OK?" She was skeptical.

I had asked to bring the Yellow Peril because its seats were more comfortable, and its tires new.

"Sure."

It was only half a lie. The infusions of coffee made me feel like a spring lamb. And the scapular hid my hand when I clutched my belly, trying to quiet the thing that was grubbing around inside.

I knew now I wasn't dealing with "stress" or a figment of my imagination. The cockatrice—for it felt as if I'd swallowed a serpent's egg—Cockatrice at last had showed itself, or rather, I discovered evidence of the damage in the shower.

I was soaping my bottom when I felt something that shouldn't be there. Incredulous, I examined more carefully.

It was the end of my cervix.

In its efforts to enlarge its hegemony and rule the roost, Cockatrice was intent on extruding my uterus.

But for the moment the pain had passed, and I unaccountably felt prepared for whatever might happen next.

"I phoned Eddie's kids," said Muskrat. "It was easier from the house: little Eddie, Joe, an' Sheila. They'll meet us at the hospital; so will my kids."

Like Rod, Jan was a nurse; Jan's husband, Gerry, was a nurse, too.

"At least we'll have enough nurses on hand to manage. Maybe your brains haven't deserted you after all."

"More'n you've got," Muskrat snorted.

"Tell me about Eddie's kids and how they're going to take it."

"I dunno. Little Eddie will be all right, I guess. Joe might be a problem. He has epilepsy, not bad, but when he gets upset he can sometimes have a seizure. The one I'm really worried about is Sheila. She got hysterical at Lizzie's funeral."

Eddie's kids met us in the lobby: Little Eddie, over six feet with his father's coloring, yet very unlike him; baby-faced Joe, heavy and soft, and Joe's dark petite wife, Ellie.

"They won't let us in. Eddie's shoutin' for you."

We hurried down the corridor. Muskrat broke into a run. An anguished roar burst from Eddie's room as she opened the door and went in.

I took Joe and Ellie by the elbows (Little Eddie wasn't the sort you took by the elbow) and propelled them back to the lobby where we could sit down. We made small talk until a wide, comfortable-looking nurse found us.

"You can see him now," she said kindly in a thick Austrian accent, and led the way to Eddie's room. I hung back, not wanting to intrude.

Muskrat came out looking rueful.

"Last time he was ambulatory. He don't understand about bedpans an' was embarrassed an' ended up messin' hisself. That's what all the hollerin' was about. They've cleaned him up now, an' he's alert. He's askin' for you."

Having quickly run out of things to say, Eddie's grown children were shuffling beside the bed. When we came in, they went to its foot and sat down.

Eddie watched us come through the door.

There was an odd half smile on his face.

Eddie was welcoming Maggie, but he was also welcoming Death.

I leaned over and kissed him on the forehead. He nodded at the drips running in both arms and tried to look cross-eyed at the oxygen tube in his nose.

"Got me trussed like one o' them turkeys."

"Never mind," I said, "I'm glad to see you."

"You hangin' around?"

"For the duration. You can't get rid of me."

He grabbed my hand.

I held it a moment, then exchanged mine for Muskrat's and pulled over a chair for her to sit on.

"We got twenty years, honey," came the insistent refrain.

Muskrat picked up a sponge and tenderly wiped his mouth inside and out.

I retired to the far corner of the room by the window and wedged myself in.

For a little while, Eddie seemed to be taken with the novelty of his situation, and was bent on keeping the conversation going.

He talked about the truck he was going to buy, and the boys eagerly joined in, egging him on. He talked about trips he wanted to take, and people he wanted to see. But every once in a while, he'd look toward the corner where I was sitting and wave at me, curling the fingers of his hand, a curious gesture, as much beckoning as greeting.

When the house physician who had admitted Eddie arrived, Muskrat and I went into the corridor for a conference.

"We've pumped him so full of antibiotics he can't have a bug left alive in his body. Now it's a matter of seeing if he can survive the weakness caused by infection. You brought him just in time, but we can't make any promises."

Muskrat asked him to notify the specialist, and we went back into the room.

Eddie was tiring.

Taking his hand, Muskrat leaned over.

"Try to sleep, won't you? We're here. We won't leave you."

Eddie closed his eyes.

I lodged in my corner.

The boys and Ellie became restless, wandering in and out until Muskrat suggested they find some lunch in the hospital cafeteria.

"You have to eat, too," I reminded her.

"I'm not hungry."

"When your kids get here, I'll sic 'em on you."

"When my kids get here, I promise I'll take a break. What about you?"

"I'm fine for the moment. Do you need anything?"

"As a matter of fact . . ." She gave me a list of things she'd brought that were still in the pickup. I went to collect them. As I was returning, a thin dark-haired woman wearing a red dress stopped me.

"You must be Maggie."

"Guilty. You must be Sheila."

She dragged at my arm and burst into tears.

"Oh Sister . . ."

She obviously didn't care if I were Roman Catholic, Anglican, or Buddhist. I was a nun, Eddie's nun.

". . . Oh Sister, I'm so frightened."

I took her back to the truck. We sat inside and talked.

"When I saw Lizzie I couldn't stop crying. I don't want to get like that again; I don't want to see Dad sick, but I know I'll hate myself if I don't tell him good-bye."

"He's not dead yet, he's very much alive, and he's resting quietly. There's no sign of sickness except that he's in bed, and there are a few tubes. Can't you just pretend you've surprised him at home?"

"Oh God, no, I hate hospitals. They're so grisly, they give me the creeps." She was almost distraught.

"How 'bout some coffee?" I offered, wishing I'd thought to lace it with Compazine.

"Gee, thanks, yes."

I poured her a cup. "I've had so much coffee I feel like I'm swimming in it. You take your time."

We sat in silence while she sipped it.

"Do you think," she began, "do you think I could just look at him from the door and if he's asleep tiptoe away until he wakes up? I'm such a coward."

"That's a fine idea. You can gradually get used to the idea of him in bed, and we can tell him you're here. You're not a coward. It would be pretty odd if you weren't afraid. These are the awesome parts of life we're trying to cope with now."

But of course that wasn't the way it worked out.

Inside the hospital doors, meeting her brothers, she began to tremble. When she opened her father's door, she burst into loud crying. He woke and tried to reach his tethered arms up to her.

Muskrat quickly took Sheila in hand. As soon as she'd had a word with Eddie, she gave her to the boys to take to the lounge. She quieted Eddie, the sound of Sheila's keening receding. . . .

I gave Muskrat the things she'd asked for.

We took up our long vigil.

The specialist came. He'd looked at the X rays from Eddie's admission, read his chart, and wanted to talk to us. He seemed a different person from the medical robot he'd been four months before.

I hesitated, but Muskrat slipped her hand out of Eddie's and beckoned. We stole out the door, closing it softly behind us. The doctor took us to a small room furnished with rugs, easy chairs, lamps.

"I'm afraid the prospects aren't very good. We've killed the infection, but the tumor's spreading, and he's awfully weak. What happened with the radiation?"

Muskrat choked out a little of her story. The doctor saw she wasn't up to talking about it, and after making a few outraged sympathetic noises, promised to speak to the radiologist. Then he changed the subject.

"We're going to have to ask you to make a decision," he said. "The crisis probably will come tonight, and we have to know whether or not you want him on a ventilator."

"I can't make that decision without Eddie's kids," replied Muskrat.

I went to get them.

It helped to have something to do, even if it was something as solemn as making a decision about someone else's death. The seven of us sat in the quiet room, and we were joined by the house physician.

The specialist laid out the pros and cons, careful not to load the problem either way, but cautioning us that once someone was on a ventilator, it was a complicated matter to decide to shut it off.

Fortunately, most of us had heard Eddie sound off loud and clear about artificially prolonged death. From that point of view, there wasn't much of a decision to make. We all knew what Eddie'd want. The doctor assured us that his airway would be kept clear, that he'd have oxygen to help him breathe.

The difficulty was taking on ourselves responsibility for someone else's life. While the family talked, I became aware of constraint, of old reflexes bowing to the moral arbiter. For a moment my habit wrapped around me like a chain, and I wished I could sink through the floor.

Then it was my turn to speak.

"I've never had to make a decision like this, either. And I really don't have any right, though I love Eddie, too."

There were murmurs of dissent.

"But, like you, I've also heard him say that he never wanted to be kept artificially alive. If there is anyone who revels in the *quality* of life, it's Eddie. . . . I keep thinking, what would I want for myself? Pneumonia's long been called the old man's friend. Eddie's not very old, but if it were me, and I were facing what he's facing, I think I'd rather die of the pneumonia. We don't know, of course. He may pull through. But if it were me, I'd rather let nature take its course."

There were little sighs as we realized we wouldn't go back on the choice Eddie'd already made. The boys decided that since there was no immediate danger, they'd take Sheila home and go about their business, if we'd promise to phone them.

We promised. They were glad to go.

Muskrat and I went with them as far as Eddie's door, and after they'd trooped on down the corridor, we went back inside. Eddie was still asleep. Or was it a coma? But no, as Muskrat slipped her hand over his, he halfway opened his eyes.

"Honey? Don't leave me. We got twenty years, honey."

"Sure, sure. You just take it easy and get your strength back."

"Maggie?"

"Maggie's here with us," Muskrat reassured him. "She's with us one hundred percent."

He peered from under his lids and seemed to see me sitting in my corner. He gave his little wave, and smiled so sweetly that I nearly wept. I reached over and squeezed his foot.

"I sure am here," I said. "You get some sleep so you'll have strength."

For what, I wasn't sure, but suddenly I understood that dying was a hard job, the hardest Eddie'd ever faced, hard as birthing and maybe harder, because it wasn't the effort of one life to bring another into the world, flesh born of flesh, but the less tangible, more consuming travail of life, of self, consenting to powerlessness, consenting to leave flesh behind and go into . . .

What did Eddie, a lapsed Catholic, think was happening? Far from the concerns I'd tried to express to the vicar, it was clear now that anything I said overtly about religion would be a betrayal, artificial, false. Eddie had rejected not God but the Church, the sanctimonious institution and its minions who had somehow let him down.

To love him, to reassure him of my love—and therefore God's—was all he needed, and that could be done without words. I could feel his questing, the silent battle to let go. I sat in my corner and prayed in stillness, trying to open to him all the strength and love that might pour through.

Though I'd accompanied many people through the months before their deaths, this was the first time I'd actually seen someone I love die. Yet it seemed as if I had never known any other purpose or life, as if Death were my most intimate friend. In a strange way, Eddie's dying reminded me of the first birth I'd assisted, years before.

He would have enjoyed my large hybrid Duroc and Poland China sow. He would have laughed at the appropriateness of the homely metaphor for his death.

I had watched Petunia anxiously all day long. Her farrowing was imminent. She would need help, as many highly bred domestic animals do. Her almost imperceptible signals opened a deep listening in me, listening for archaic speech, listening for a primal voice that spoke without words, telling me what I needed to do, setting my responses in motion even before I was aware I had moved.

As night fell, I turned her into the pen I'd cleaned and spread with fresh straw. Slowly she lowered her huge body to the earth and drifted into semiconsciousness. When I came into the pen with a bucket of hot water and a pile of freshly laundered towels, she grunted a little. I patted her on the haunch.

Before I could warn him away, a neighbor began to climb in after me.

Petunia half rose and made as if to charge, though I don't think she could have gained her feet. She nearly killed a man once, but I didn't feel that I was in danger.

I sat there, motionless, a clean towel gathered in my hands, ready to catch the first piglet—just as I was now sitting in Eddie's hospital room, motionless, hands cupped in my lap in the primordial gesture into which hands often fall when people pray, a gesture at once offering and receiving.

And then Petunia made a slight convulsive movement, and the first membrane-covered bundle slipped into my hands. I quickly tore off the semitransparent cover, tied the cord, cleaned mucus out of the little mouth with my finger, surprised at the needle sharpness of the teeth, and dried the soft, wriggly body with its tiny trotters.

The rust-colored, black-spotted piglet squealed as I pumped air into his lungs, and his mother answered with a soft grunt. Only when I handed him to someone to take into the house to keep warm until all were born did his squeal take on a different note.

Then Petunia became alarmed.

I soothed her, and she lay back again.

In a few moments, another piglet appeared.

Word travels fast in farming country, and Petunia's extraordinary bulk had made her famous. One by one, neighbors came quietly into the old barn, and from the darkness outside the ring of light spreading from the lamp I'd clamped to the pen fence, they witnessed the everyday miracle. Even crusty old Bullard came, and once, as I turned to hand a piglet to a waiting helper, I saw him brush awkwardly at his eyes with the back of his hand.

I went through the repetitive, ritual motions with the same Ur-knowledge that had slowly come over me in the small hours of this morning—an aeon it seemed since we staggered through the dark and rain to seat Eddie in the car to bring him here, a faint memory as we waited at the intersection of time and eternity—the same knowledge that at once seemed most commonplace, yet comprehended all the elemental forces from which true ordinariness comes forth.

During that long-ago night in the barn, I knew without knowing when Petunia needed an injection to help her contractions; something unseen nudged me so that I understood when a piglet had become stuck in the birth canal, and something told me what to do about it.

Dreaming, yet more conscious than I had ever been before in my life, I scrubbed up, knelt down in the straw, and slowly inserted my hand into Petunia until, along the warm slippery tunnel, I could feel pouches on either side. A set of minuscule hooves yanked back into one elastic mouth as the alien presence of my arm passed by.

I found the trapped piglet when my arm was in the sow up to my shoulder. If something had alarmed her then, she could easily have killed me, but there was communication between us that went as deep as life itself. As gently as I could, I manipulated the little body until it slid into something resembling a normal position. I eased my arm out, washed, and waited for the wayward child and its siblings to be born into my hands.

Now I sat with my whole being in the narrow channel of Eddie's room, waiting, waiting for his birthing, offering the only help I knew to give, knowing with the same Ur-knowledge that what was needed would be given in the strait place of his dying, and that when he slipped away from us, other Hands would receive him.

The piglets' had been a birthing into our world of flesh and sense; Eddie's was to be a birthing out of flesh into unfathomable life. As I had been caught in the rhythm of the piglets' birthing, so I was now caught in the rhythm of Eddie's dying.

Muskrat nodded as if she shared my thought. She beckoned with her free hand, and when I came over, put my hand into Eddie's as she took hers out.

She left the room, having given me her greatest gift.

It was deeply quiet. Eddie's breathing rose and fell; oxygen hissed; I.V.s dripped. The Austrian nurse opened the door and poked her head around with a questioning eyebrow. I smiled and nodded that all was well, and she left us in peace.

Minutes passed, days, perhaps, months would not have surprised me. One became another as Eddie's life was imperceptibly drawn from his body by the opening of the infinite abyss of Love, leaving his earthly bones exposed on the Western Shore. . . .

. . . Whispering in the corridor beyond the closed door, and Muskrat came into the room with her children and son-in-law. Her tired face had relaxed a little with the arrival of reinforcements.

Jan was there, the shape of a fertility goddess, reddish hair pulled back into a bun, spectacles like her mother's perched on her face; Rod, tall and spare, with the reserve of suffering, compassion, and rage he had carried since Vietnam; Gerry, Jan's husband, comfortably square, his dark, half-Choctaw face brimming with kindliness.

We embraced.

Muskrat took me aside.

"We're bein' kicked out."

"What do you mean?"

"Don't you know it's way past supper time? The kids have got us a motel room across the way, an' are insistin' we at least go an' lie down, even if we can't sleep. They'll call us if anything happens."

Jan was already sitting by the bed with Eddie's hand in hers; the men, both of them ER nurses, were checking the drips and dials, alert to the slightest margin for improvement.

The blind leading the blind, we left for the motel.

The upstairs bedroom was huge. There were tables, armchairs, a TV, and two vast wastelands that were beds. The kids had left trays of sandwiches, a bowl of fruit, soft drinks, and stronger stuff in case we wanted it, rightly guessing we wouldn't think to eat. Muskrat ate half a sandwich, forcing the other half on me as we sat facing each other, sitting on the edges of the enormous, king-sized beds.

"You go first," she suggested, nodding at the bathroom.

She switched on the TV with the remote control.

I emerged to find Muskrat lying on the far bed with her hands behind her head. The TV was off.

"All yours," I said, pulling back the spread from the near bed. I could have slept for a week.

But when Muskrat came out of the shower in her nightgown and crawled into the other bed, I was wide awake.

She snapped off the light.

We lay there, each in our vast desert of a bed.

After some time, her slightly mocking voice came through the dark.

"Iff'n this bed was much bigger they'd have to supply you with grub an' a guide."

I laughed. "Can't you sleep?"

"No."

We were silent awhile.

"This bed's too damn big and empty."

I reached over to the lamp on the nightstand between us and pressed the switch.

Muskrat lay stiffly on her back, tears rolling down her cheeks.

I flung off the covers, clambered out of my own wilderness, and lifted the corner of her sheet.

"Mind if I join you?"

"I thought you'd never get the hint. You're pretty dense, you know?"

"Yeah, but nothing like you."

"Oh shaddap."

I brought my pillows and she slid over.

We both lay on our backs without speaking.

Finally she asked the ceiling, "How come it's takin' him so long to die?"

"Well," I sighed, moving my hands slowly to clutch my belly in which Cockatrice had begun to squirm, "maybe he's hanging on for you."

"How come?"

"Well, even though we both know better, you've always let him feel he's been responsible for you, let him think he told you what to do even though you do what you want, let him worry about your safety and so on, and now maybe that's pulling at him and keeping him from going."

Muskrat pondered this.

"Yeah, I guess you're right. But what can I do to help him let go?"

The memory of a phone call about a monastic death rose slowly to the surface and broke.

"I don't know, but maybe you have to reassure him, give him permission. You haven't talked directly about death with each other, have you?"

She shook her head. "Not since that first day. We've been too close. I keep kickin' myself that I shoulda brought him down here sooner."

"No point in that. You said yourself he would have squawked if you'd tried."

"That's true. Go on about this permission business."

I told her about the nun who died.

"The abbess said she just couldn't seem to die, and then one morning they asked her, can you wait until after Mass for a last Communion and blessing. The abbess had finally realized that this nun had been so obedient all her life that she was waiting for permission to die. 'So,' said Reverend Mother, 'I gave her permission to die, and Jesus to take her.'"

"Eddie ain't no nun."

The thought of Eddie in a wimple was too much.

"Yeah," I agreed when we'd caught our breath. I took her hand, "but the principle's the same. You two are vowed to each other. Maybe he needs you to say that you're OK, that you'll be all right, that it's fine for him to go, and you love him no matter what."

Muskrat considered this. Her bleary eyes dribbled water. "I'll do it when we go tomorrow." She began to sob. I took her in my arms and she wept on my shoulder.

"Thank God you can cry."

She held on hard.

Then through her tears, "A dew exberience."

I plucked a tissue from the box on the nightstand and handed it to her.

She blew.

"Let's try to sleep now. Do you want me to stay?"

"Yeah, if you don't mind an occasional shower."

Sleep claimed me instantly, deep, black, dreamless sleep. I awakened only when Muskrat bumped against a chair as she was dressing.

"Damn," she apologized, "I didn't want to wake you up."

"I would've been mad as hops if you hadn't."

"Well, since you're awake, get your duds on an' let's go."

"You ought to eat something."

"We'll get some coffee at the machine."

She picked up a tired sandwich and a bunch of grapes. "You want anything?"

I shook my head.

We ran into the house physician just outside Eddie's door.

"He's a little better this morning," he said, before we asked. "We had to start suction last night, but it wasn't too bad. . . . Of course . . ."

"Of course he may be rallying just before he dies as people often do," Muskrat finished the sentence for him, not unkindly.

He nodded, not ungratefully, and we left him standing in the corridor.

Jan was sitting by Eddie, holding his hand. She was hollow eyed and unkempt.

"The boys are sleeping in the lounge," she explained. "We took shifts."

I looked down at Eddie, lying motionless, not seeming to breathe. His skin shone with silver transparency. He seemed stymied somehow, or perhaps he was gathering strength. Whatever it was, everything seemed to be on hold.

But there was also the certainty—how, I don't know—that he was near death. Muskrat and Jan talked softly while I stared at the dying man. Then I went over to the corner.

People drifted in and out.

By this time, we were weary beyond all measuring. The only bad part was the suction. The inhalation therapist came and sucked out Eddie's nostrils and throat with a vacuum tube. The procedure obviously irritated him much more than the mucus did, and I wondered if he really needed it.

Why can't they just leave him alone?

I sat and poured all the strength I could into the body on the bed. Concentration twined the threads of my tired being. The words of commendation began to sound of their own volition in my heart:

Go forth, O Christian soul, out of this world;
In the name of the Father who created you;
In the name of Jesus Christ who redeemed you;
In the name of the Holy Spirit who sanctifies you.
May your rest be this day in peace, and your dwelling place in
the Paradise of God. . . .
Receive him into the arms of your mercy . . . into the glorious
company of the saints in light. . . .
May angels lead you into paradise, Eddie. . . .

The prayers had their own life. Some, I realized, when an unfamiliar phrase would float by, must be prayers Eddie learned as a child.

Jesus help, Mary pray.

I left the prayers spinning.

≈≈≈

In the early afternoon, the house physician came in to look. He took Eddie's pulse and left.

A few moments later, the Austrian nurse came in and said quietly, "The doctor thinks about three hours now. . . ."

She paused. Her eyes wandered over the room to rest on me.

"Sister will know."

What will I know and how? I've never seen anyone die before. . . .

But I did know. We all did. We could sense the last effort when it began even though there was no perceptible change.

Jan went out to phone Eddie's kids.

We all sat immobile, straining with the immobile man on the bed, begging for him to be able to let go, silently encouraging him, mentally unclasping the fingers that so stubbornly held on to the last scrap of life as he had known it.

Suddenly the door opened.

Two bright young things in pink-striped student nurses' uniforms entered and announced chirpily that they were going to turn Eddie and change the bed.

Everyone was horrified, transfixed.

I felt myself rise out of my chair and go over to the door. When I was nearly touching them, nose to noses, I said in a voice I'd never before heard, "That's not necessary. Please go away and leave us, and ask everyone else to do the same."

They looked uncertain, mumbled something about a supervisor, disappeared.

When the invisible struggle became unbearable, Muskrat glanced at me, gathered herself, and leaned over to speak into Eddie's ear.

"Eddie, it's OK to go," she said, barely containing her voice. "I'll be all right, honey, I promise. Don't you worry about anything. I love you. I'm with you. We're all with you. You're all right. It's going to be all right. You just relax an' let go."

I don't remember what else she said, but he did seem to relax a little.

Little Eddie and big Joe came quietly into the room.

All at once, together, we noticed his breathing was slowing down. As if raised by a single hand, the seven of us went over the bed, each grabbing on to a piece of Eddie to give him what strength and comfort we could to ease him out of life.

Rod, so ambivalent about death, Muskrat had told me, despite his emergency room nursing, (or perhaps the cause of it), did something that shocked and delighted her. He went up to Eddie's head and told him who was in the room, each of us by name.

"We're all here," he said, "Muskrat, Little Eddie, Joe, Jan and Gerry, Maggie, and me, Rod. We love you. We're with you. We'll take care of Muskrat. Don't worry about anything."

The pauses between breaths became longer. The angels and saints, responding to many invocations, were almost tangible.

As I saw his life draining out of him in all its mysteriousness, my own life, so tightly bound now to his dying, tugged hard at its moorings. I ached to go with him.

Oh! Eddie, I want to go, too! Take me with you, please. . . .

Suddenly I was afraid he would hear me, but then understood that there was no turning back the ebb tide that was fast receding, leaving us stranded, even as I ran behind it down the beach. . . .

. . . O God, let me go, too. . . .

. . . as Eddie drew one last quiet breath and exhaled slowly and long, slipping away from us into endless light.

〰〰〰

We wept, embracing one another, huddling together.

Muskrat's children began doing the little services that were their prerogative: removing the drips, taking out tubes, putting Eddie's teeth back in, making slight adjustments to his body, already composed and at peace.

Muskrat moved to the far corner and stood there looking out the window, cussing softly. I put my arms around her. She cussed a little louder, and wept. When her tears subsided, she said, "I wish we could just take him home an' bury him."

"We could. We just have to do it in twenty-four hours."

"How do you know?"

"Had to find out about burying a monk once."

"Well, we can't. He's to be buried with Sally, an' I have all the information here somewheres. . . ."

She was rummaging around in her purse when Sheila burst into the room, weeping and crying. She screamed and collapsed over her father's body. Little Eddie looked about to explode; tall, pear-shaped Joe just stood there, bawling like an infant.

Then, one by one, we said our good-byes—his forehead was already cool under my lips—and went out into the corridor where the *gemütlich* nurse and house physician were waiting for us. They took us to a quiet room.

Muskrat found the papers she'd been looking for, and suddenly we were all floating a bit, lightened from our grief, released from the very real, yet unreal, world in which we'd lived for the last few days.

We all became a little goofy.

I thought Little Eddie was particularly goofy when he came through the crowd, backed by Joe and Sheila, to ask me if I would do the funeral on the following Saturday.

"Don't you want me to find a priest?" I wondered if later they'd regret not having had a requiem. I also dreaded a new confrontation with the vicar.

"No!" Little Eddie was a thundercloud ready to spit lightning. "We had one for Lizzie's funeral and it was horrible. You were his priest; you're our priest. It's you or nothing."

It would be very wrong to say no.

"I'm very honored," and I was, "but you should know I've never done a funeral before."

A WASP Anglican nun conducting a Mass-less funeral for a Portuguese Roman Catholic family surely was possible only in these ecumenical times. It would be my last and best gift to him, and to Muskrat. But his family needed to know I was inexperienced.

"We're not worried."

I found Muskrat and murmured in her ear.

"Let's get out of here."

"My kids are taking us to supper."

I made a face.

"They're tired, too. It won't be long."

It was late afternoon and winter dark when we left the hospital. We were the only customers in the brightly lit coffee shop. Gerry was as punchy as any of us, and started the nonsense by teasing the waitress who came to take our order.

Our laughter quickly got out of hand, inciting Jan and Rod to take up an old game from childhood. They glared at each other saying, "*My* mother, *you're* adopted," fighting to sit in her lap, in spite of the fact that each of them was at least twice her size.

Then with medics' gallows humor, they began to imitate Muskrat's former patients, surrogate sibling rivals from the past, gibbering and twitching. Having the restaurant staff for an audience only egged them on, and by the time our food came, we were limp. It was shameful, but we laughed anyway.

Muskrat's sense of propriety made a bid for attention. "Seems like we ought to be weepin', not laughin' like this."

Jan jumped on her. "Eddie would hate us to be sad. He'd love it."

Muskrat saw the crazy logic and her anxiety subsided.

"You're right," she admitted after a moment, "he would."

And we started on stories about Eddie.

But for me, the moment of intimacy had passed. All I could think about was the long solitary drive back to Hunter that would give me time to absorb a little of what had happened. When the party broke up, I turned down Gerry's offer to take me home. Jan would take Muskrat in their VW, the Silver Slug.

"You sure?"

"I'm sure."

"Well, phone me when you get home."

I set off alone into the night.

Next morning, when I finally came to, I wondered how I'd ever make the hour's drive to the vicar's, much less conduct a funeral in two days' time. He would hear about this funeral from the gossip machine, no matter what I did. I might as well go and get it over with.

Beyond this, I knew nothing of the protocols of funerals and funeral homes. I'd only been to one funeral outside a church in my life, and that one was Orthodox Jewish. I'd never had sole responsibility for a large public service, and while I wanted to take it on and felt sure I could bring it off, the vicar's expertise could make all the difference in the confidence with which I moved in an alien milieu—if only he would share it.

Whatever his faults, he was a good liturgist in any setting. He had the information I needed: how to keep the funeral professionals from intruding their slick plastic substitute for grief into our homely sorrow; how to keep their banalities from diluting the mystery of mourning. I also wanted a second opinion on the order of service I'd worked out during the journey home the night before.

I wondered how hard a time he would give me. He had a short fuse, a ferocious, explosive, sometimes violent temper.

I didn't announce myself ahead of time.

I drove slowly along the wet roads, past the silent vineyards, row upon row of brooding shadows, past my old farm, past Bullard's, on into town.

Cockatrice was ominously silent; its presence forced me earthward.

"What can I do for you?" asked the vicar, not happy to see me on his doorstep again. He didn't invite me in.

"I need you to tell me the protocols for doing a Roman Catholic funeral in a funeral home. Everything we hate, open casket, etcetera."

I was too exhausted to pussyfoot around. Besides, there was no point.

The vicar's face clouded.

"I thought I told you to get a priest."

I held my emotions at half halt, reins strained to taut threads.

"They won't have one. I told you that. When they asked me, I suggested it, and they said Eddie's mother's funeral was so horrible they wouldn't dream of going through that again, that it was me or nothing. I told them I'd never done a funeral before."

Why does his rage force me to explain myself?

"It isn't right," the vicar pronounced.

I am not going to ask you to take over.

"Why isn't it right? They have said in so many words that I am their priest. . . ."

You never knew Eddie; you didn't go through his dying with us; you weren't Death and Truth to him; you didn't keep vigil at his bedside, or comfort his family, or help them with the life and death decisions we had to make. . . .

". . . and I won't let them down."

I was too tired, too sick to argue further. I would not let him invade the intimacy of our suffering, or tell us we had no power to bless each other or our dead. I would not betray my friends. I felt my heels digging in.

He saw it.

"You're intransigent."

"Yes."

He stood there, silently threatening.

I was implacable.

Finally he sighed, "Come inside."

When we were sitting down, he actually thawed a bit. Finding no way around the problem, he decided to help me. At least I wouldn't disgrace the Church on his account.

"Let's start by you telling me what you have in mind."

We went through the service I'd planned. I read the homily notes.

He approved everything, trying to hide his surprise, made one or two good suggestions.

Once he decided to be helpful, he told me everything I could possibly need to know. Most useful of all was his insistence that the body was given into the care of the Church, that the undertakers were there to exercise specific, practical skills, not to take over.

He missed the irony of his own words.

"You have to make it clear that you are in charge, you represent the Church, and you won't stand for any nonsense. Phone them ahead and spell out what you intend to do. When I have to do one of these, and I don't agree to do them very often, I always lead the coffin to the hearse in procession with psalms, stand beside the doors until it's in, and shut them myself."

These were the cues I needed, and I went home with a sense of commission. Why did it take so much unneccessary agony to unclench the official fist?

Before I picked up the phone I went over again what we had discussed, and what I intended to do.

I rang the funeral director, found out what the family had ordered, announced my intention to take charge.

"Did they ask for a rosary in his hands?"

"No."

"Do it, please."

"It's not on the order."

"I take full responsibility."

From what Muskrat had told me, I knew this had been a detail of Lizzie's funeral. I was sure in the anguish of the moment the family had just forgotten. In their own way, they were deeply religious, and the old symbols meant a lot.

Then I took a deep breath, and my courage in my hands. I was the Church, and I was in charge.

"Another thing. None of this artificial carpet and little sanitized packets of dirt."

"It's in the order."

"Who put it there?"

"It's standard."

"Well, it's not *our* standard. Take it off the order. Please have shovels at the grave side. We will give anyone who wishes a chance to help cover the grave."

There was a gasp at the other end of the line.

"I'm not sure the unions . . ."

"I am quite sure you can arrange it," I interrupted, letting the iron that had been solidifying somewhere in my heart sound in my voice.

He was defeated. "Anything else?"

"No. I'll come early to make sure everything is in order. Thank you."

I hung up first.

I did get there early, but mourners were already gathering. I prepared the thurible, hung it in a safe place, and went to find Muskrat. She was in the corridor talking to a youth-not-yet-man whom she introduced as her grandson.

"Jeffy would like to help."

"Have you ever been an altar boy?"

He shook his head, "Just tell me what to do."

I explained the thurible routine. He was alert and intelligent, and I had no qualms until out of the corner of my eye I saw him come out of the parlor, his face swollen from the tears that soaked his collar.

By this time I was talking to someone else. I wondered if he would be able to go through with it. I managed to break away and go to him.

"I'll be OK when the time comes," he answered my unasked question, fighting his fear and his adolescent awkwardness.

And he was.

Little things stick in the memory from such occasions, not only Jeffy's alert, composed assistance—"He became a man that day," Muskrat told me later—but also the feeling of the body's cold, stonelike flesh under my lips, the nauseating close-up of the makeup artist's tarty skills.

Why can't they leave well enough alone . . .

I knelt off to one side until the crowd finally sorted itself out, sat down, stopped fidgeting and talking.

Smoke rose in spiral clouds as I censed the body in the open coffin.

Perhaps it was that sight that made me emphasize in the homily that it wasn't Eddie we were burying, but his body. As the service began, I felt the congregation's mute pain that made even the most ancient and familiar responses impossible—and a lot of them had never been inside a church.

So I said them softly myself, accompanied by a few hesitant voices. Then a few more joined in, until finally, when we got to the Our Father, everyone who wasn't weeping grasped thankfully at the familiar words.

I began the homily.

We reverence Eddie's body because for a time it housed his life that is so inextricably woven with ours. . . .

It was the altar on which Eddie, in his own way, made the offering of his life. . . .

Now, like a spark in the stubble, God has kindled Eddie with divine love, and his death has brought him to the fullness of the vision we all seek, however blindly, each in our own way. . . .

To grieve for the dead is a holy act. . . . Don't hesitate to weep. Tears enable us to let him go, ease our heart's understanding, and our helplessness in the mystery of death.

There may be some of you here today for whom these gestures and prayers are empty, or even alien. If so, do something for Eddie's memory, and name it your mourning.

Take a walk on the beach, celebrate a task you particularly associate with Eddie, perhaps a skill that Eddie himself taught you: clean a generator, fix a car, chop wood, laugh with his great laugh, love life with his wide love. But bring him to mind, because it is not only through the tangible gifts he gave us that he is still among us. . . .

Then the Kontakion, the beautiful prayer from the Orthodox liturgy with its Alleluias, the sprinkling, and I was leading the bier through the warren of corridors to the hearse.

Christ our passover is sacrificed for us. . . .

The canticles and psalms resonated with startling loudness off the smooth walls. People arriving for other funerals stopped to listen as our procession moved slowly past. Life inherent in the words sounded them, the slow chant filling every hallway and corner.

Listen, all you come here to mourn. . . . Listen, all you who loathe these tawdry fashions that cheapen this great and holy mystery. . . . Listen to the grandeur of the life we share, the Love beyond time and comprehension . . . freedom we are too frightened to allow to possess us. . . . Listen. . . .

I closed the hearse doors firmly on the coffin and got in front between the director and the driver, the psalms still echoing in my body. The hearse eased out into afternoon shopping traffic.

I didn't want to talk. I needed to hoard what energy was left, to be replenished from the pool of silence from which the psalms had sprung.

They resumed as the coffin moved the short distance between the hearse and the grave.

Loud crying from Muskrat, Sheila, and another woman, who were sitting in folding chairs, eyes and mouths open. Their sobbing pulsed with a rhythm as old as women weeping over their men.

The grave was sprinkled, the coffin lowered, the prayer of committal said, the invitation offered.

The shovel took up its task.

As the first clods hit the coffin, the wailing resumed. Hands passed the shovel, one to another; people presented themselves with the same dignity that was part of Eddie's dying to the end.

Over by the chairs, we reached for one another's hands; the loud and public grief became the quieter, deeper tears women share among themselves.

When the last volunteer had heaped clay on Eddie's coffin, a near absolute silence fell.

Time halted.

Muskrat reached for my arm, and I helped her from her chair. We headed for the limousine.

"Let's get out of here," she muttered. "Let's go home."

The Worm Turns

Whether Cockatrice was subdued by the solemnities surrounding Eddie's death, or whether I had been too preoccupied to notice, the fell worm decided to make up for lost time. Three days after we buried Eddie, Muskrat, my nice Jewish mother, was driving me in the Yellow Peril through a steely downpour to see my nice Jewish doctor.

"You look like hell," was the tactful way she put it.

Not to take this lying down, I responded in kind.

"So do you."

"I gotta reason."

"So do I."

"Yeah, but I know all my reasons an' you don't. Now get on the phone and make an appointment."

By now I knew something really was wrong, so I did as she ordered.

At the end of the hour's drive, I was soaked in sweat. My hands were icy, numb. I felt as if I were in someone else's body.

"You look like hell," said Richard cheerily. One swift diagnostic glance spiked his greeting with concern.

We'd known each other for more than a decade—I was still farming when he first came to town; we'd become close friends. He wore Eastern polish, Long Island accent, healing presence, easily on his big frame.

"Thanks," I snuffled, too miserable for jokes.

"Here, have some coffee," he handed mugs all around, "and while I'm at it, how about some antifreeze."

To my astonishment, he pulled a flask from his desk drawer.

"This is a full-service office," he explained pouring brandy, "and you two look as though you need more than doctoring. My first prescription is a cup of kindness, and then we'll find out what's wrong with you."

As we sat in his study, the warm brown pottery comforting our hands, the fiery liquid our insides, Muskrat told him about Eddie. It was the first time she'd really been able to talk since the funeral, and I was even more grateful to him for risking this extraordinary departure from regular clinical practice.

When we had drunk up, he herded me out of his study into the examining room.

"Now," he said when I'd stripped and was shivering on the table in a flimsy gown, "what's going on?" He was the sort of doctor who wanted the context of a life, not just the symptoms of a body.

I told him about the events of the past six months. I told him I'd had one infection after another. . . . Finally, I told him about Cockatrice.

"Any one of those things is enough to set something off. Dammit, why don't you take care of yourself? Have you thought about two weeks in a warm climate?"

I laughed, "You gotta be kidding."

"I'm not kidding. I mean it. Two weeks—no, make that a month—in a warm climate."

"Frankly, I don't think I could make it that far. Anyway, you know I don't have any money."

He was taking my pulse and blood pressure. He listened to my chest.

"Lie back."

He had barely touched my belly when pain ripped through me, forcing out a scream.

Richard turned white as his coat.

"Let's have a look. I'll try not to hit a sore spot again."

That was all he did: look.

"I'm not going to examine you. Sit up."

I had the second shock of the visit as I obeyed.

Tears runneled his face. He half turned away, then swung back violently, reaming me out because I hadn't come to see him sooner, because of pressure people were putting on me, because of all sorts of things that had nothing to do with anything.

"I want you to go next door and see the surgeon."

"Huh?"

"I'll call him myself."

"What are you talking about?"

"I'm not sure. That's why you have to go to see him."

Before I could say anything more, he marched off to phone.

Under my medical smock, something chewed at my guts.

Surgery had never crossed my mind.

And then I became aware of how thoroughly everything but Eddie's death had been shoved from my consciousness, aware of a tiredness that suffused every cell, tiredness that flooded through me like a sea change. . . .

A sea change.

The memory of poisoned words and breached defenses bubbled up and dissolved.

So, Cockatrice was the foul child of that awful day years ago, nurtured by conflict that had thrown me between fire and water in ensuing months. But there was no point in blame. . . .

. . . That forgiveness was my first reaction, and that it came so naturally and simply, after all the months of searing anger, was, that day, the biggest shock of all. . . .

But I had no time to reflect. Richard took some blood samples, and bundled me next door.

"If you examine me," I warned the middle-aged, brown-haired surgeon, "I will rise up from the table like Lazarus. It hurts too much."

I sat across the desk from him, curled over my pain, trying through the haze of disbelief to make rational decisions, to reply to the questions he was asking in his midwestern twang.

He took me seriously; his examination was cursory. "We'll use sonar after we admit you."

He commented on this and that, waiting for me to catch up with him. The diagnosis became crystal clear.

"And while we're in there, we'll have to take a look around to see if there's anything else going on that's related, so we'll make a vertical incision. . . ."

Over the stream of reassuring clichés, we measured each other. He wondered how honest to be. I wondered if I could trust him. Richard had said, "I'd trust him with my wife." Richard's wife was his treasure.

But in the end, tired of euphemisms, wanting to make my own medical decisions, I had to fight.

"I want to go through this only once, so please take everything that might remotely cause a recurrence. And another thing. . ."

I wanted him to know I wouldn't be humbugged.

". . . I won't have chemo or radiation. . . ."

He started to interrupt, but I cut him off.

". . . I have a book to finish and I can't write if I feel lousy. So if worse comes to worst and you can do something about pain while you're in there. . . ."

"What's the book on?"

"Tears."

"We'll keep that in mind. . . . You don't have any funny ideas about drugs, do you?"

"If you mean, will I refuse painkillers, the answer is definitely no. That would be a masochistic ego trip of the first order. But I don't want to be on them any longer than necessary. I don't want to get hooked."

"You won't get hooked if you have that attitude and you're taking them just for post-op pain. . . . I'll phone you as soon as we're on the OR schedule."

Under the hard practicality, Muskrat's words came back: *I feel like I'm speaking lines and watching at the same time.*

After we were back in the pickup we just sat, watching the rain sluice over the windshield.

"He said I'd better see my lawyer. His office is just a couple of blocks from here. Go back to Main Street and turn left."

Muskrat turned to me, her ancient green nylon vest rustling against her plaid flannel shirt.

"God damn it," she said slowly and clearly, pain naked in her smudged eyes and blanched face. "God damn it, don't *you* die on me."

Eddie's face against the pillows appeared and disappeared.

O God, I want to go too. . . .

Tears came now, welling of their own accord.

"I can't make any promises."

<hr>

Three mornings later, when I woke up, I couldn't get out of bed. Or rather, I tried, and knew I'd better not attempt the ladder without someone there to steady me. Fortunately I'd brought the phone up into the loft. The conversation was abrupt.

"Can you come?"

"Be right there."

Pomo looked up from her nest as I put the phone down. She half growled, half whined. I tried to reassure her. Kelly already lay with his back against the foot of the ladder. The twenty-five minutes seemed like hours.

Muskrat's feet sounded on the porch. She opened the door and called up, "I'll walk the dogs first." She snapped on their leashes, dragging them outside.

Her head appeared at the top of the ladder. She looked down at me with mock disgust.

"Give me your jar."

"Listen, that's really above and beyond. You just stand at the bottom and steady me as I come down."

"Oh no you don't," retorted Muskrat, "I'm not volunteerin' to be steamrolled if you slip. Now gimme that jar."

She took it, and as she bustled around the cabin, I started to cry.

"I'b so sorry. This is the last thig you deed dow."

"Will you shut up? What do you think I'm goin' to do with my time, now Eddie's gone? I'm just as glad to have somethin' to do. But dammit," her head reappeared at the top of the ladder, her gaze fierce, "dammit, don't you die on me. Now what do you feel like eatin'? I gotta go to town an' shop."

"I don't feel like eating."

"You gotta eat."

"I'm not sure I can."

"Well, use your imagination. If you felt like eatin', what would you eat?"

Guilt spread through me like rising damp.

"Out with it."

"The only thing I feel like eating is expensive, but then, I don't feel like eating much. . . . A little crab and a few stalks of asparagus and some dark beer to settle my stomach."

Muskrat guffawed. "You can take the hermit out of San Francisco, but you can't take the San Francisco out of the hermit. Anyway, pregnant women always want weird junk to eat, even when they're big with what you got. I saw crabs in town yesterday, dirt cheap. Anything else?"

"No, I don't think so. . . . Oh yes. Some of your cheap novels, some postcards. There's money in . . ."

But she was already halfway out the door.

"Don't you try comin' down."

≋

Muskrat moved in. She brought a mattress from her trailer, and sleeping bags. She slept on the floor. Pomo, knowing a good thing, burrowed in with her.

In the hour of first light, I looked down from the loft.

A large and a small head lay on the pillow; the tip of a hound's tail peeped out from one edge of Muskrat's sleeping bag. Kelly lay across her feet.

Each morning after the dogs were walked and she was sure I had everything I needed, Muskrat would leave. "You need your time alone, I know," but her exquisite intuition always brought her yellow car hurtling back down the hill just as the pain got bad, or the silence oppressive.

She knew I needed time to sort things out in my mind, to write my friends to beg prayer. The handwriting scrawled across postcards: "Tumors found. Surgery February 8. Please pray. I'm a coward about pain, but I want to make an offering of this."

It was the third week of January. I was humiliated by my fear, but a long history of physical pain from illness and accidents gave me good reason to be afraid. Bad as the pain was now, it was nothing compared to what would follow surgery; the post-op pain after this sort was legendary.

After several days Muskrat observed, "You got to have a hospital bed. You're gonna fall off that ladder one of these mornin's an' kill both of us."

"I can't afford it."

"I heard there's a hospice formin' up here. Why don't you phone 'em?"

She gave me the number she'd copied off the bulletin board at the general store. The RN who was forming the hospice came over. She was pregnant, too, but with a real baby.

"We haven't really begun yet," she told me, "but I think you can get a bed from the Lions' Club. They supply them for any kind of illness. Let me know if you need anything else, and I'll see what I can do."

We had a bed in twenty-four hours. I was down from the loft, sitting in one of the rice-straw chairs with a dog on each foot, when the two Lions' Club men brought it.

Their dismay was evident, not only at the remoteness of the cabin, but . . .

I hadn't looked in a mirror for days, but they killed any curiosity I might have had. At the same time, they made me feel as if it were an *honor* to supply me with a hospital bed.

"Just let us know when you're done with it," was all they asked.

They said it to Muskrat, not to me.

Although the bed took up half the floor space in the

cabin, it made things easier for humans and animals alike. Muskrat wasn't under as much physical strain, and the dogs stopped their nervous pacing. I could lie in bed and watch the fire; my books were at my fingertips.

Evenings became a kind of game.

"How many teaspoons of crab you want tonight?"

Cockatrice was enlarging its borders, and the pain had become generalized.

I was down to two stalks of asparagus, a teaspoon of crab, half a beer.

"You gotta eat," Muskrat would insist.

"I can't. I'll urp."

"Well, at least drink some beer. There's nourishment in it."

One night when we were going through this versicle and negative response, my empty stomach growled. I looked down at my belly, bulging with Cockatrice.

"Quiet, junior," I commanded.

Muskrat had the grace to laugh.

Phone calls and letters trickled in, promising prayer and asking for prayer. To be asked for prayer in my condition was a new experience. Something in my upbringing had made me think that if you were sick there was something morally wrong with you. I knew better, but I'd never been able to shake the feeling.

Now someone was telling me that my helplessness, dependence, pain, were precious.

"If there is room in the prayer of your pain," one letter read, "please remember me." A high-flown theory flapped softly home to roost.

"Are you afraid?" a caller asked.

"Not of death . . ."

How could I be afraid of death after what I'd been through with Eddie and Muskrat? Death was my best friend. Muskrat sensed I was content to go. But I began to realize that I was also content to stay. It no longer mattered which. . . .

". . . only of pain . . . I'm a real coward. Please pray."

Evening blanketed the cabin. I lay half dozing in bed, watching flames play around the coals. Muskrat sat in my desk chair reading a novel with the help of a clamp-on book light.

Pomo was in bed with me, her sinuous body stretched out full length along my right leg. Sometimes she reminded me of a cat more than a dog. She was quick as a cat, too, when it came to mice. Kelly lay under the bed where my right hand, dangling between the rails, just touched his back.

Without looking up from her book, Muskrat asked, "How're you feelin' about it?"

"Mixed."

"Mixed-up?"

"No, it's all terribly clear, somehow. I just don't know what to choose."

"What do you mean, 'choose'?"

"Well, when Eddie died . . . when Eddie died, I wanted to go, too. . . ."

"Yeah, I knew that. . . ."

". . . and then it seemed my life had come to an end. I mean, there was a sense of completion, as if I had done in life what was important to do, and I was free to go. I still feel that way. . . .

"I guess you've probably figured out that with all the broken agreements, etcetera, I've decided to leave here. I was going to tell you. After. I figured we could get all our mourning over at once, instead of going through one bit and then having to go through the whole process two or three more times. It just isn't my vocation to defend someone else's property, especially when that someone is as irresponsible as the parish is both to the property itself, and to this community."

"It isn't going to get any better after you leave."

"I know. But there's nothing more I can do. I'll speak to them again, if . . ."

"If . . ."

"I feel I'm being offered a real choice. I feel that if I chose to, I would die peacefully under the anesthetic, and this would be all right with God, that God would let me. It's almost as if God will choose what I choose. That's what I mean by a real choice. To die on the table would be a terrible thing to do to the doctors, and even more, to you. But I feel that it's a clear option, and if I choose to die now, I will. But I don't trust my motives for wanting to take that option."

"Why not?"

"I don't know, but I think it must have something to do with my vows. It's as if God is giving me the opportunity to grasp my life and my death, and yet, while that would be OK, God also is offering me something else, something I can't see, something . . . something that would be even more costly than what I've been through. Part of me just wants to rest forever. I know that's a silly idea, because I don't think being with God is that kind of rest. . . .

"But if I chose to live . . . if I choose to live, it may be that what felt like dedication and commitment in the past would prove only a beginning; life would mean a stripping beyond anything I have experienced or can comprehend now, even death itself. In a way, death would be a *relief*, and I'm not sure that's what I'm committed to. And I worry about being afraid of pain, being lazy, taking the easy way out, stuff like that."

"So what are you going to choose?"

"I don't know yet. I think maybe I'll give the choice back to God. That's not a cop-out. I'm choosing. But if I do that, then I've relinquished the last bit of control over the direction of my life that I might subliminally want to retain, the kind of control that shuts out God in preference to my willfulness, my restricting and restricted perspective. I think that's important."

"I don't get it."

"You know all the torment I've been through since I came, what I've been battling to resolve and forgive."

"Yeah. . . ."

"Well, that day at Richard's, I was shocked that all I could think about was somehow getting word to all those people who worked me over in one way or another that it was *all right*. Not that what they did was all right, or the damage, or the anger that's been both necessary and unnecessary—all that has fed whatever it is that's growing in my belly.

"Instead, after all these years of conscious struggle, I found to my astonishment that on the deepest level, in spite of my thoughts and feelings, the thing is already resolved, that some kind of profound transformation has begun, out of sight, in the dark. That's a comfort, really. You always wonder how you will react when you come right up against death. Now I know. Now I know what I have long suspected, that God takes our hearts' assent and leaves the conscious stewing to camouflage real change that's happening necessarily out of our reach. I guess I feel that in giving the choice back I'm making a commitment to live on that level; to trust even when everything conscious points to not trusting; to know that God is at work under the apparent level of absurdity, as long as I'm willing. Does that make any sense at all?"

"Too much sense."

Cockatrice evidently didn't like all this talk of God and death and choices, and gave me a solid kick in the midsection.

"Don't talk about it anymore now," said Muskrat, pulling herself out of her chair and jerking a hankie from her hip pocket to wipe the tears I didn't know were flowing from my eyes. "Try to get some sleep. It's only a few more days, and you want to build up your strength."

I nodded and gulped.

"You want a pill?"

"I think I'd better. . . . Muskrat?"

"Yeah?"

"You're a nurse. Will you go into the lab for the gross dissection so I know what it looks like? I asked the doctor if I could have a look, but he said they have to do it while I'm under."

"OK, if they let me."

"And be there when I wake up?"

"If I can."

"Promise?"

"Promise."

"Know what?"

"What."

"I'm afraid I'll cuss."

Next morning when I woke up, I had a queer feeling something was different. I lay there, puzzled, then with growing bewilderment, as I became aware that my fear of pain had vanished.

I was incredulous and skeptical.

Hah! Just wait until it really *starts to hurt!*

Thus do we receive miracles.

It was some hours before I was able to absorb the enormity of this gift, but Muskrat saw immediately when she brought me some weak tea.

"You look different this morning."

I wasn't quite sure how to tell her.

"This may sound weird, but I don't think I'm afraid of the pain any longer. Maybe it's pre-op denial or something, a euphoria that will disappear when the chips are down. On the other hand . . ."

I tried to distance myself from my self. The earth seemed to shift under me, only this time it settled firmly into place. No longer was I disoriented by the unreality of fear.

". . . On the other hand," I went on, trembling for the vastness opening up before me, "all of what's happening to us has become quite ordinary; it's been that way all along. Even though the really hard part for me begins three days from now, it just doesn't matter in the scale of things. It's as if everything is equally precious, Eddie's death, everyone's loving-kindness, the illness and pain. I don't have any desire to keep any of it, to hang on to any experience. This must sound slightly crazy. . . ."

"No," Muskrat busied herself behind my head in the kitchen alcove, "somethin' *is* different. I can feel it. We'll just have to wait to find out. Maybe we'll never know."

By afternoon, conversation was forgotten. I slipped in and out of sleep. The three days wandered by. . . .

I managed to rouse myself enough to walk, painfully and unsteadily, to Muskrat's car, her firm grip on my elbow and around my waist.

The original plan had been that I would have tests, then go back home to return for admission the next day. But as we drove slowly along the misty road that curved through the vines, winter naked, with their canes tied cruciform to the wires, we both knew my condition was too poor to make a second journey.

The surgeon saw, too.

"I think we'll put you in today. We'll call it an emergency admission so there won't be any problem with the insurance."

Then . . .

"Can you last until the day after tomorrow? We can schedule emergency surgery. . . ."

I nodded, too drained to speak.

"The hospital isn't busy right now, so we were able to get you a private room for the rate of a semi."

I blessed him. I had braced myself for the impact of people all the time.

The room in the little country hospital was a surprise. The walls were papered with a Victorian print, furnished with a period wardrobe and cabinets.

I crawled thankfully into bed; whatever happened would happen.

The night before the operation, an old friend, a writer, came to see me. He laughed when he saw the room. After we'd visited awhile, he read us a satirical story he'd written about his sexual coming of age. He didn't spare himself, his

pubescent silliness, or anyone else, and Muskrat and I laughed so hard that the nurses came in to see what was happening. It was the best possible pre-op therapy, even though it prompted Cockatrice to savage me.

Next morning I woke up hours before I needed to, wondering if the vicar would bring Communion.

Then I was distracted by the little medical things that needed to be done. They approached, happened, fell away.

There was a sedative; then the last hurdle, the one I'd most I dreaded, the catheter, proved to be nothing at all. I must have looked as wry as I felt because the nurse remarked, "Everyone thinks it's going to be awful. Never mind."

The gurney arrived. I was lifted on, wheeled into the freezing OR. The circulating nurse snugged a hot blanket around me.

The young blond assist, whom I'd never seen before, couldn't wait to begin. To focus his energy, the solid, quiet Hispanic anesthesiologist told him to deaden my arm with saline. The assist complained pompously that the syringe wasn't marked.

Fine time to argue about your protocols.

The anesthesiologist did it himself without a word, and after a moment or two, deftly slid a cannula into my vein.

"I feel funny."

"I slipped you a mickey."

His quiet laugh began to recede.

I waited drowsily in the warmth.

This might be the last moment I could speak.

I had no desire to speak.

Everything had been said from eternity.

If I were to enter the next phase of life, so be it.

I wondered, a little, that I was unafraid. . . .

I lay there, wrapped in warmth, suspended. . . .

The gurney began to slide forward, rushing faster and faster. I was leaving these kind strangers. It would be rude not to greet them even as they slipped past my eyes. In my languor I tried to puzzle out whether it would be more polite to say good-night or good-bye. . . .

III

The Fullness of Mercy

The air is not so full of motes, of atoms, as the Church is of mercies; and as we can suck in no part of air, but we take in these motes, these atoms, so here in the congregation we cannot suck in a word from the preacher, we cannot speak, we cannot sigh a prayer to God, but that that whole breath and air is made of mercy. . . .

If I should declare what God hath done . . . for my soul, where he instructed me for fear of falling, where he raised me when I was fallen, perchance you would rather fix your thoughts upon my illness, and wonder at that, than at God's goodness, and glorify him in that; rather wonder at my sins, than at his mercies; rather consider how ill a man I was, than how good a God he is. If I should inquire upon what occasion God elected me, and writ my name in the Book of Life, I should sooner be afraid that it were not so, than find a reason why it should be so. God made sun and moon to distinguish seasons, and day, and night, and we cannot have the fruits of the earth but in their seasons; but God hath made no decree to distinguish the seasons of his mercies. In paradise, the fruits were ripe the first minute, and in heaven it is always autumn, his mercies are ever in their maturity. We ask *panum quotidianum,* our daily bread, and God never says you should have come yesterday, he never says you must come again tomorrow, but *today* if you will hear his voice, today he will hear you.

If some king of the earth have so large an extent of dominion, in north, and south, as that he hath winter and summer together in his dominions; so large an extent east and west, as that he hath day and night together in his dominions; much more hath God mercy and judgment together. He brought light out of darkness, not out of a lesser light; he can bring thy summer out of winter, though thou have no spring. Though in the ways of fortune, or understanding, or conscience, though have been benighted till now, wintered and frozen, clouded and eclipsed, damned and benumbed, smothered and stupified till now—now God comes to thee, not as the dawning of the day, not as in the bud of the spring, but as the sun at noon to illustrate all shadows, as the sheaves in harvest to fill all penuries. All occasions invite his mercies, and all times are his seasons.

—*John Donne, LXXX Sermons, 1640*

Raven

Drift fiery lapped pain bright . . .
Woman compassion talking . . .
Ear itch . . .
"Maggie, cough. Take a deep breath and cough."
Idiot . . .
Bath floating pain dazzle . . .
Muskrat . . .
"Muskrat . . ."
"Who's Muskrat?"
Secrets . . .
Order pain surge . . .
"O . . . pain . . . bare feet . . . migrant . . . shot . . . cold
. . . tried warm . . . loving . . . Muskrat!"
Rack . . .
"Don't . . . sorry . . . shouldn't . . . promised . . .
Muskrat!"
Murmuring . . . coughing.
Male voice.
"She's not doing any good here. Let's take her to her
room."
White-hot toss chop.
Corridors . . . spinning . . .
Bumps.
Richard's voice . . . kindness' sake . . .
Body lifted . . .
Soft . . . wooly? . . .
. . . sheepskin!
Pain body . . .
"Muskrat."

Richard . . . steps . . .

Hall outside—O joy . . .

I took my first deep breath, nearly fainting with pain.

"*Muskrat!*"

"You better get in there."

Richard.

Muskrat hurried to my bed.

"Hesh! Quit cher bawlin' and bellerin'. I'm here."

And she was. She sat down and took my hand.

"Now you behave."

I opened my eyes, tried to smile, but the alien body revolved.

Shut quick.

She scolded, "You don't have to look so smug just because you got what you want."

"Where . . ."

"I was in the lab like you told me. Everything's OK. There's only one tumor they have to check by section, but even if it's malignant, it's encapsulated. Them doctors just stood there shakin' their heads. They don't understand. They were sure."

She picked a piece of ice from the bowl on the nightstand and dribbled water into my aching mouth.

Breath . . . stink . . .

"Prayer . . ."

"Yes, you're damn lucky. Now take a deep breath and cough."

I shook my head minutely. "Can't."

"Malarkey," scoffed Muskrat, "you don't think I believe you after all that bellerin' do you? You do as I say."

Eyes still shut, I tried not to laugh.

"Hurts."

"I know it hurts, but you have to get that gas out an' your lungs workin' again."

A tentative breath, a tiny cough.

My eyes flew open. Pain passed beyond my body.

"Why . . ."

Words were still hard to find.

". . . why pain in back? Expected front. Why back?"

Muskrat, who'd had similar surgery, replied, "I dunno why they never tell you about it. There's a bundle of nerves near your spine they have to cut, an' I expect that's what's hurtin' so bad."

Anxiety.

I shut my eyes again.

"Babbled about you. Sorry."

"You couldn't help it," she consoled. "Don't worry. Them nurses hear a lot of stuff an' know how to keep their mouths shut."

I wasn't all that sure.

"Did I cuss?"

"No, you didn't cuss."

"Anybody here in the room?"

"No, we're alone now."

"Then shit."

Intense pressure.

"Shit, shit, shit, shit, shit . . ."

Muskrat laughed.

"Seems like I heard that before. OK, I agree. Shit. But you're gonna be all right."

Tears were pouring from her eyes into her open, laughing mouth.

≈≈≈

I found a nurse surveying me.

"I'm going to put my arm under your back, and you're going to sit up and dangle your legs. And then, if you feel OK, you're going to stand."

Who was this lunatic?

"You must be out of your mind."

She was amused. "That's what they all say. Come on."

Before I knew it, I was sitting up, dangling my legs. I stood. Normality flooded.

"See? What did I tell you. Tomorrow we'll walk you. And the next day you can take a shower. . . ."

O bliss, a shower!

". . . and after that you must walk whenever you feel you can."

It was on one of those long walks, taken often during sleepless nights, that I saw Richard reading a medical journal. He was sitting in a chair tilted against the wall outside the ICU. It must have been two in the morning. He didn't see me.

He was still there at breakfast time.

I stopped to say, "You were in my room when they brought me back from Recovery."

The tired man didn't try to hide his delight at seeing me up and about. "I wanted to be there."

During the long afternoons, I would lie on my bed watching the rain splash down on the parking lot, emptied out by pain, and by something less tangible. I had no words for it. Sometimes the gratitude would wake me in the night, weeping.

I remembered the requests. Prayer poured through the pain, supporting me; I was without desire. The humdrum hospital routine, the messy little details that attend healing: itchy stitches, gas, getting your innards functioning again— each sharply outlined, joyous, transient.

The day was coming when I would have to go home and take up life again. An unknown quantity stretching before me would take some getting used to, more difficult than the idea that I might not have awakened.

I burrowed into the present.

There was a TV in the room. I felt well enough to see the Winter Olympics, most particularly Torvill and Dean, whom I'd never heard of until I switched it on.

The narrator told the story they were to dance.

The two lovers swirled out onto the ice. The world looked on.

They hung suspended in a great gliding arc.

At the apogee of this endless, swinging curve, facing each other, Dean took Torvill's face in his hands, leaned over, and kissed her, leisurely and deeply, as if indeed they were the only two people on the lip of a volcano.

I wept.

Whenever I see a photograph of this moment, it all comes flooding back: the pain, the hospital bed, the rain outside, the dim light from the table lamp, the music, the colors moving on the TV; prayer, love, support, trust, my illness, my whole life, summed up in that extraordinary kiss.

The next day someone mentioned home.

I looked out the window at the filthy weather and hoped for a reprieve.

Muskrat arrived.

I asked if they were sending me home.

She shook her head.

"I haven't heard anything."

I suspected complicity when no one mentioned it again.

Suddenly it was time.

When can I go. . . .

━━━

Muskrat had the freshly shampooed dogs tied up until I was in bed and settled. We had a joyful reunion.

It was good to be back, but the cabin was no longer home.

I had no home, nor were there any claims on me. What I had suspected was true: if I thought my life had been given away before the surgery, surely it was now no longer my own.

For a time I was full of awe.

Then I was mad at God.

"Post-op depression is a reality most people have to deal with," Richard pointed out when I asked him about it. "After all, it's an invasive procedure, a kind of violation."

The word reverberated faintly in the back of my mind.

"I can give you something, or you can increase the dose of hormones, but frankly, if you think you can, I'd just as soon you ride it out and go through whatever you have to go through."

He was right. His word became an obedience.

I had no call to be angry at God, though I knew God wouldn't mind. I had freely given back the choice: I had been given life in return. Perhaps I rebelled at my own extravagance. Deep inside I would have it no other way.

I might have rebellions in the future; there would be times when old injuries would come back to haunt me. I might have nowhere to go, no certainty, but all the better: this was the mirror of Love's self-emptying, offered in the hard facts of my life.

I could accept or refuse. I was free to explore.

One morning it was time to live alone again. Before I could say anything, Muskrat's voice floated down from the loft.

"I'm goin' today."

"I was just waking up to the fact that it's probably time."

"I'll come down an' help you with wood an' things, but you need to get out an' walk the dogs yourself, now, an' start doin' little chores. Anyway, I'm worried about Rachel. She's been coughin', an' it looks like I may have another nursin' job."

Neither of us was prepared for the shock of separation after so many weeks of sharing death and life. Neither of us was prepared for our failure to recover autonomy. In spite of Rachel's pneumonia, Muskrat would find time to drop by at least twice a day, sometimes more often.

She'd bring a meal on the excuse that she had to make sure I ate. Or, if she disappeared for what seemed an impossible amount of time, I'd think of an excuse to phone her.

We didn't talk about it.

I got rid of the hospital bed. The same men came. They marveled at my health and well-being, as if I'd been called back from the grave—which I had.

Having the cabin back to normal helped to shake off

convalescence. It wasn't long before I was taking walks for fun, slow, careful walks to be sure, but I could make it halfway up the road, and soon all the way to the top of the ridge.

We had a real spring that year—spring for the first time in many seasons. The wildflowers were spectacular. We emerged into the sun, the flowers and I, blinking with new life. Each day I ventured a little farther.

There were more wood orchids than even Muskrat could remember. Mission bells were easy to find, a stalk of scalloped umbrellas the size of my thumbnail, purple on the outside, speckled yellow inside. There were whole slopes of blue and white flags far up the creek near the wilderness area, and once I found a yellow lily.

It was the first spring of my new life. Each petal and leaf impressed itself as I walked slowly, or knelt dumbfounded with a trowel in my hand.

Golden eagles, back from their winter vacation, circled overhead, screaming; ospreys returned to their huge brush pile of a nest downstream; otters feasted on a late run of fish.

I planted seeds and strawberries, raising and lowering myself carefully, rejoicing at returning strength. It rained enough to keep things growing.

Steelhead splashed up the creek, thrashing in their gravel nests, spawning, rushing back to the sea. I was caught again in the wonder of death and life, a state of unknowing—of the old world, of my static, now shattered, notions of life and self.

What did all those people feel—Jairus' daughter, the son of the Widow of Nain, Lazarus? Did they, too, wake to unknowing, to the dread of life without fear? A newness, the vastness of life not their own?

We pray presumptuously for miracles, not realizing the consequences, without pity for the poor victim. We speak glibly of resurrection.

Are you ready for resurrection? Don't believe it for a minute. No one can be ready. Maybe we can prepare for death, but it is infinitely more difficult to prepare for life. I had been told that full recovery from my surgery could take up to two years. But I now knew that convalescence from the gift of life would take the rest of it.

≈≈≈

The long spring faded with June's heat.

Evenings, I'd walk the dogs to the ridge to catch the breeze blowing off the fog bank that blanketed the coast.

On one such evening, with the cabin still in sight, I spotted a vulture sitting to the left of the road, staring intently at something on the opposite bank.

Its naked head thrust outward on a long sallow scrawny neck. It was so preoccupied that it didn't see us until we were just a few feet away. Then it sensibly flapped into a nearby madrone.

Vultures are cowards: they like their meat very dead. This one was waiting for something to die.

Now I am very fond of vultures, and while I didn't wish to deprive this one of its supper, at the same time, if the intended meal still had some life, I wanted to give it every chance. Either that, or dispatch it. I tied the dogs to a fence post and crossed the road to investigate the small black something on the fern- and poison oak-covered bank.

The pile of feathers staggered and flopped. When I reached down, it bit me hard with a black beak that was at least half the size of its body. When I persisted with my attentions, it threw itself silently on its back, claws up, in a posture of submission—or so I thought until it grabbed my thumb again as I reached down to lift it.

Its breastbone was lean as a turkey carcass after Thanksgiving dinner, but its spirit would fight to the last breath. Nearby lay a headless lizard, brought by one of the worried parents who were flying around from tree to tree, signaling quietly. But it was obvious that by this time such delicacies were indigestible, and their care inadequate.

With apologies to the vulture, I tucked the formidable little bird under my arm and went back to the waiting dogs. They drooped, dejected, their walk aborted.

They seemed to know that this small change of plan was only a hint of the disruption to come. They heaved great sighs. The new addition would mean sharing, readjusting the pecking order.

As we walked downhill in the green-gold evening, the fledgling quieted.

. . . and feed the young ravens when they cry. . . .

So far this one was silent, but I was soon to know the plangent, haunting cry of a hungry, frightened, lost raven, torn between wildness and its adopted "flock," half-educated in the ways of ravens, half in those of humans and dogs.

When we reached the cabin, I fed them and opened a can of tuna. I offered some to the little black fiend, who squirmed and fought and bit. It was too young to eat on its own, or, more likely, it was just stubborn. It didn't respond to a tap on the side of the mouth that stimulates other fledglings to open up.

I knew I had to get some food and water down it, and soon. I couldn't do it alone: you needed one hand to hold it, another to pry open the beak, and a third to force-feed.

I phoned Muskrat.

"Come see what I found."

"Humph," snorted Muskrat, "what is it this time?"

"You'll love it," I wheedled. "Just come and see. I need you to help feed it."

Muskrat was a sucker for any creature. She would go on for hours about Bosco, a wild piglet she'd raised as a member of the family until Eddie put his foot down and exiled the hundred-pound porker to a pen.

"*Now* what are you getting me into," she yelled, and hung up.

In twenty minutes she drove in.

When she saw the droll little bird, her face melted.

"I need you to hold it while I feed."

She looked wary.

"Here." I handed her some leather gloves.

She put them on and reached for the youngster, who promptly grabbed her thumb and twisted.

Muskrat, grimacing, cooed, "You ornery little shit."

She was hooked.

When it had eaten enough, it shook its head violently, spewing tuna over its surrogate parents in a sticky shower.

I put it in a small cage I'd found in the shed, until I could nail some netting around the porch. It would need to have exercise to strengthen it until it learned to fly. When it had settled in the cage, we got our first good look.

The right leg was badly twisted. It looked like a hip injury. The wing drooped on the same side. We couldn't tell if it was down to help the bird balance as it tried to stand, or if it, too, was injured.

We discussed taking it to the vet, but figured the trauma in its starved and dehydrated state would be too much. Better get it strong and then see how the injuries were healing.

For three days Muskrat came down four times a day to hold the struggling ball of feathers while I parted its beak and stuffed in food and water. On the fourth afternoon we were fed up.

"I'm sure it's time for it to eat on its own," I said as she picked it up.

It had become used to us and sat quietly in her hand. I held food out.

Over its face came a reflective, oddly reptilian look, as if it were remembering something. It reminded me of an iguana I'd once kept as a pet: a million years gazed out of its yellow eye.

And then, as if it sensed we were at the end of our patience, the little raven grabbed.

Set on the floor, she snatched and gulped, took a sip of water, tilting her head back to let the liquid trickle down her throat.

We congratulated the bird and ourselves. Muskrat said she'd be back for supper.

It was hot that evening. Muskrat brought beer. We were sitting on the porch waiting for our food to cook. I had just fed the dogs, Pomo inside, Kelly outside. He had his nose in his king-size pottery dog dish.

Raven was walking now, testing the world with her beak, pulling things to bits for fun. I hadn't fed her yet, but she made the connection between her new skill, eating, and the big dog slurping in the corner.

She marched over to his dish, which was five times her size, squatted down and gawped. Whether she was begging or threatening I don't know.

The wolfish beast, ignoring her, continued to inhale his food.

Raven was not to be ignored. She rose, reached up, clamped her sharp mouth on his sensitive ear.

Kelly leapt back with a roar of pain, outrage, surprise. Raven sampled his dinner, decided she didn't like it, wandered off. Kelly gave me a bitter look, went to the farthest corner of the porch, flopped down.

We tried not to laugh. But the incident was more serious than we knew: not only did Kelly not eat the remains of his dinner that night, he also lost his place in the pecking order. Raven was now Number Three, and for the rest of our time together, she and Pomo were engaged in a power struggle for Number Two, and sometimes she jousted with me for Number One.

Raven became bolder.

Another evening, Muskrat and I were sitting with plates of fish in our laps. Raven was at our feet. We weren't paying much attention to her until she grabbed Muskrat's trouser leg, flapped, and splash-landed in her supper, snatching some fish, sending the rest flying as she skated for a foothold in the melted butter.

"She *smelled* it," Muskrat expostulated, while I doubled up. Then it was my turn to be attacked.

After that, we tried to teach her some manners.

<hr>

It was Raven who taught me how to live again.

Mornings I'd let her out and sit with a book while she did her exploring. She had started bathing in Kelly's water dish, so I bought a large dishpan for her bathtub.

She would stand on the edge, sample the water to see if the temperature were to her liking, dip her head, then her shoulders, then jump in with a loud thump, sending showers of water every which way in a fine spray as she thrashed her wings, shimmied, scooped water over herself.

When she was done, feathers draggled and pink skin showing, she'd perch on a chair to preen herself in the sun, falling into a trance, sometimes going to sleep.

One morning when she woke from her nap, the reptilian look crept over her face again. Before I could move, she spread her wings and clumsily flew.

Twenty-five feet between the cabin and the tree, she was mobbed in midair by jays. I shouted, scattering them long enough for her to grab at a bough about fifty feet up. Under the impact of her unpracticed claws, it refused to stay put. She slipped down through the branches, grabbing desperately for a hold with wings, feet, beak.

Finally some matted twigs stopped her fall. She sat there, panting. When she took off for another fir, I covered my eyes.

Young ravens stay with their parents for a long time after they start to fly, and the parents teach them everything. I'd seen a pair educating a youngster in the big field on top of the east ridge early one autumn when I'd been cutting wood.

Since I couldn't fly, I could only pray that Raven would be guarded by the God of falling sparrows. Flying is a *learned* skill—that was obvious.

It was only a matter of time until she got lost. Like any parent of a wayward child, I was frantic.

I rang Muskrat, who was philosophical.

"You've got to let her go. One of these days she's going to go wild, you know."

"But she's not ready yet; she doesn't know anything; she's not old enough."

This was in the morning. By late afternoon, my throat was hoarse from calling. I kept hoping the echoes would reach her wherever she was stranded.

Muskrat phoned.

"Is that you callin'?"

"Yes," I croaked, "I still haven't found her."

"Well, if she's anywhere around, she can hear you. I thought somebody was hurt in the woods."

I hung up and went out on the porch. It seemed I heard a dim cry, but I'd been thinking that all afternoon. I called again anyway, and walked up the road. Flapping awkwardly down the ridge through the woods, landing frequently, came a frightened, hungry, adolescent Raven.

She squatted in the forest litter. I crept up the bank with some food in my hand.

She was breathing hard, eyes fixed and unseeing. She backed away from me, too scared and exhausted to recognize anyone. After a moment, she snatched the food. I closed my fingers around her beak and drew her to me. Her trance broke, and she sat contentedly on my wrist while I took her home.

The very worst moment was the morning after her first overnight roost in a tree. I was late getting her inside. Instinct was too much.

When the light hit a certain angle, she flew to a big fir near the cabin, preened herself, then hunched into her nighttime stupor. Nothing could wake her or persuade her to come down. Hoping she'd chosen a branch where a raccoon couldn't surprise her, I went uneasily to bed.

At first light I came out and began to call, offering breakfast. She looked at me on the porch, calculating distance and angles. As she flew, my heart stopped. A red-tailed hawk had been waiting for this moment, and as the awkward young bird flapped toward me, it dropped to intercept her.

At the last possible instant, Raven saw Death stooping, and tilted one wing. The heavy raptor, too clumsy to make a countermove (thank God it wasn't a Cooper's hawk), continued its earthward plunge, while Raven landed trembling on my arm.

She began to wander, but always would come at my call. It was grief to her that I could not fly. She tried to entice me, accepted my disability, went alone.

She loved walks, and when I'd take the dogs up the road, she played touch-and-go on Kelly's back. He got so he'd tolerate it, but Pomo would snarl after a certain amount of tormenting.

It was only one day when I was checking her for ticks that I understood why: every time she alighted on Pomo's back, Raven would grab the tip of an ear. She had bitten them bloody.

I started carrying a water bottle with me to squirt Raven when she misbehaved.

I had to train her to stay out of the garden, too. She loved to shred flowers, to pull green tomatoes off the vines.

I'd turn the hose on her when I saw her land there. She learned to obey me—up to a point.

She played touch-and-go on the dahlias and zinnias.

She'd waltz through the air of the clearing, watching me out of the corner of her eye. When she was sure I was looking, she'd brush the petals with her feet, turning her head to mock me.

She'd also sneak into the garden from the creek to pull off what tomatoes she could reach from the ground. As long as she left me some fruit, I pretended not to notice.

Each day held for her the delight of the first morning of creation, Wisdom at play before the Face of God. She wanted to do whatever I did, and when that didn't interest her, she would go off on her own to dig and plant, poke and pry, excavate, explore; creating, destroying, discovering, making mischief.

She would steal something and watch my reaction. If she thought I wanted it back, I'd never see it again. She'd bury it, or take it high in a tree, tuck it into a hole, or the crook of a branch. But if I feigned indifference, she'd drop it and try to steal whatever did interest me. If I still pretended indifference, she'd bring back what she'd first stolen, and if that seemed not to matter, she'd go off in the woods and bring back a "present," an acorn or a bit of foil, holding it in her beak.

I would grasp it, she would pick it up again, then offer it, finally flying off to stash it in a secret place. She made me understand that this exchange of gifts was very important for her social development. This was all very well, but I was careful to keep things I valued—like the car keys—in the house. It was clear why Noah threw the raven off the ark first.

Strength was a long time returning. Often I'd sit by the creek with the leashed dogs beside me. One day I tossed a twig for the ever-expectant Kelly. I was still too tired for a real game with large sticks flung hard on the streambed for him to leap after, find, bring back.

He always had to find the exact stick you'd thrown. He was obsessed. Chasing sticks was his sole reason for existence. He would bring a stick to anyone who visited, merry brown eyes flirting an invitation, jaws champing the wood in his mouth, be it twig or stove wood. Pomo didn't really like to play fetch, but in order to get her share of attention, she'd dive after the quarry.

Raven was exploring under some leaves when I started to toss the bits of wood, but she immediately came over to watch. Without warning, she, too, chased a twig, outpouncing both dogs.

Pomo pretended not to care. Kelly tolerated her for a few more throws, but, while he was below her on the pecking order, invasion of sacred stick territory was just too much.

He waited for his moment. When finally she tried to snatch the twig he was guarding between his large and hairy paws, he sent her flying, *bap!*, tail feathers over teakettle, with just enough force to keep her from recovering in midair, but not hard enough to hurt her.

It was Raven's turn to be outraged. She got to her feet with every feather upright. I threw twigs for each of the dogs, then threw one for her, just to see what would happen. She retrieved it. I threw for her again; she brought it back.

But playing fetch wasn't as much fun as thieving, and after a few more rounds, she got bored. She went off a little way with the twig I'd thrown her, mumbling it in her beak. As I watched she lay down on the leaves, rolled over on her back, juggled it between feet and beak.

I built her an aviary, and locked her in whenever I went out in the Yellow Peril to keep her from flying along behind and getting lost. She didn't seem to mind, but she was always glad to see me return, to be released. She perpetually tried to sneak in the house to dig in the pile of papers on my desk, to torment the dogs. She wanted to be wherever we were.

When I sat on the porch she would stand for long minutes on the back of my chair, tenderly preening my hair strand by strand, working her way forward until she reached my eyebrows. Her massive beak worked more delicately than an embroiderer's needle as she picked each tiny hair and smoothed it into place.

But when she reached for my eyelashes, I gently told her to stop, miserable at my lack of trust. Muskrat had told me too many wild stories about ravens and eyes.

Raven had a sixth sense about what I was doing. Whenever I sat down during the day for still-prayer, she'd fly in from wherever she was playing. While I sat inside, she perched on her open aviary door. She had discovered it would swing if she rocked back and forth, and my stillness was daily accompanied by the music of a softly squeaking hinge and Raven's crooning. Sometimes she sang herself to sleep.

She was discovering the powers of her voice. She loved to startle me with strings of whoops, whistles, sirens, human voices, bizarre calls of her own invention. She'd imitate the cry of the pileated woodpeckers. She delighted in fooling the big black and white, red-headed dimwits. She'd call them to a meeting, and while they dodged from tree to tree, unable to figure out why they had come together, she would mock them, laughing and chuckling at their bewilderment.

She took it on herself to alert me when anyone came on the property. She seemed to know where the boundaries were. When Leticia was coming, she would fly downstream to greet her long before she announced her presence by our two-note halloo.

She began to talk with other ravens, but it wasn't until autumn that they accepted her to fly with them. It was then that Muskrat caught her and a friend stealing eggs from the duck pen. Muskrat was sure it was Raven because she saw the Department of Agriculture ring on her right leg, and the yellow plastic chicken ring on her left. We'd banded her shortly after she started flying.

There weren't many trespassers that summer, but when I went out to investigate someone on the crossing, she would swoop low and buzz them. It must have been unnerving to have a large black bird appear out of the forest to knock your hat off.

The LSD castle had visitors almost every weekend. There were regulars, including one group of families with young children three to seven years old who had come for several years at summer's beginning and end to stay in the big old house in the trees. They had visited just before I found Raven, and during the summer, a baby was to be born.

I wrote the mothers about Raven. "She is very young and still learning her limits. She's intensely curious, but has never seen children. She'd never knowingly hurt anyone, but I thought I should let you know in advance so that the children can be prepared."

I wondered what would happen when they met.

The children arrived on Friday night of Labor Day weekend, packed in the backseats of the cars with their tired parents and a hundred miles of road grime. Raven was already asleep.

In the morning, I let her out as usual to play. No one was around.

A little later I heard shrieks from the direction of the god-in-the-rock. I ran.

The children and Raven were at play. The humans were cowering on the ground in front of the house, giggling, while Raven watched from a nearby branch.

Then the children jumped up and ran behind the house to the big rock with the beetling face. Raven followed, swooping low. The children screamed in mock fright, their faces radiating delight.

They ran toward the creek and threw themselves on the shingle. Raven swooped again, cackling. She brushed three tow heads with black silk taffeta wings.

I crept away.

All weekend they romped together. As soon as she woke up on Sunday, Raven went down to the big house to tap on windows until she found their room and called them out. Monday morning the tired children slept late. She gave up and flew away.

But she hadn't gone far.

When Mark, aged six, came out and didn't see her, he flapped his elbows, cried, "Caw! Caw!" and was rewarded with the sound of wind rushing through outstretched black primaries, and a torrent of joyous Raven babble.

They went down to the creek again—they lived in the creek that weekend, the three children and Raven—digging sand and loading Tonka trucks, tossing pebbles and rocks into the water with much loud splashing.

Monday was a perfect end-of-summer day, hot, but a cold wind blowing. The adults started packing the cars; the children were kept inside.

When it was time for them to leave, Raven was on my cabin porch, unraveling my weaving. As they rolled by, the children leaned out the windows.

"Good-bye, Raven!" seven-year-old Daniel cried.

"Caw! Caw!" called Mark.

Raven was too preoccupied with her destructive task to respond.

I had no inkling of a problem until I went down to the big house to close the valve on the propane tank. Raven went with me, as she always did, and it was then she realized the children were gone.

She took off from my wrist and began to tear around the canyon, ricocheting off sheer walls, diving among the trees, buzzing the stones of the creek, crying like a mad thing. Finally she returned to me, landing hard on my arm, beak open, panting, crazy-eyed.

I wept that wildness would choose to know such sorrow.

She trembled, her shining deep blackness reflecting every color in the failing light, feathers all awry.

"Raven," my words were hoarse as her gutturals, "Raven, I do not know the way to comfort you."

I took her back to the cabin and put her into the aviary for the night.

The next morning was laden with foreboding when I let her out. She was morose. She flew briefly around the canyon. Then she disappeared.

When she hadn't returned by nightfall, I was distraught. She was still young and inexperienced; her flying had become more agile, but she didn't yet know how to navigate by flying high and looking down. When dawn came, I began to phone; the general store, the school—any place a lonely raven might look for children.

In the late afternoon, Dan's wife phoned. Her CB, tuned to the local channel, was always on.

"I hear you're lookin' for a raven."

"I sure am."

"My daughter, Madge, has her up at the forestry station near the conservation camp where she's cookin' this summer."

The camp was a long way up the ridge north and west of

Hunter, but I hoped I could get there before nightfall. The dogs and I jumped into the pickup.

She had already gone to roost when we arrived, but from Madge's description it had to be Raven. From her account, we were able to piece together what had happened.

Raven had gone hunting for children. It took her a day and a half to find her way across the ridge to Hunter. She landed at the edge of the village where two toddlers were playing in front of their bungalow.

Terrified by the enormous black bird that tried to join them, they fled inside—only to find it had followed. Raven flew up onto the kitchen table and demanded food from Mother.

Fortunately the woman realized that Raven was someone's lost pet, tired and hungry. Not having heard my SOS, she got in touch with Madge, who took the waif under her care. Now Raven was roosted for the night; there was no point in hanging around.

Muskrat, the dogs, and I were back by first light the next morning.

I started to call her.

Raven flew to a nearby tree. She had the same, dazed, frightened look she had the first time she got lost. With a little more light, she flew straight to us.

She stayed pretty close to the cabin after that, venturing farther afield only after she'd learned to soar. Then she'd join the local flock at their convention in the thermals over the canyon.

Or sometimes she'd ride the wind alone until she was a black speck far overhead. When I'd call and she didn't come immediately, I'd look up to see her dropping out of the sky.

At the ridge tops, she'd start swinging in tight spirals until she landed proudly on my wrist. Then she'd reach up with her rapier beak, and, laying it along my neck under the jaw, make soft baby bird noises.

I would burst into tears: who was I to call wildness from heaven?

Muskrat was visiting the day Shirley rode her horse

over, her Brittany spaniel trotting at their heels. The dog was trained for hunting pheasant, but she'd never met a bird like Raven.

We were sitting on the stoop. Shirley stood nearby with the reins in her hands. The spaniel sat politely on the ground near her feet. Raven was puttering around close by, pretending to look for things under leaves, while sizing up the strangers. My dogs were locked in the cabin because Pomo was jealous.

The first little rush Raven made to pull the hairs on the spaniel's tail surprised us as much as it did the dog.

Shirley told her to stay.

Emboldened, Raven rushed in and pulled the tail itself. Hard. Then the hairs between the dog's toes. The spaniel was utterly bewildered. Slowly it dawned on her that this abuse was supposed to be play. She got down on her forepaws for a rough-and-tumble, and woofed.

We held our collective breath as they tangled. But we weren't prepared for Shirley's horse. Tired of being left out of the fun, he began to toss his head and stamp. Shirley thought he was just restive and spoke to him, but Raven knew, and made a rush at his fetlocks. Pretty soon the three animals had a game going that had the three humans completely stumped.

"We are very lucky," Muskrat finally murmured, breaking the spell, "seein' the things we have."

But this idyll couldn't last forever. With autumn, Raven began to mature. I had to hike the property boundaries with Eric, the local forester, to find surveyors' marks in preparation for the logging the parish had arranged.

Raven went with us, nervous about staying down in the brush. Sometimes she'd ride on my shoulder or arm; then she'd fly high to get a fix on our location in relation to the cabin. When we'd stop to rest or make a note, she'd join us on the ground, tugging at our bootlaces, or yanking on our jackets. Once she began to court Eric, and it was then I knew for sure she was a female.

She ate less and less of the food I put out; she had begun to hunt. She'd gulp a few mouthfuls in the morning and stash the rest, beakful by beakful, under logs and leaves, or in the forks of trees. One day a half-stunned wild pigeon—stooped on by a hawk?—flew erratically through the clearing. Raven was on it in a blink, pulling it apart even before she'd killed it, a puff of feathers floating to the ground. She might as well have been shredding a flower.

And the day she brought me a present of a bloody shoulder blade from some small animal she'd found in the woods, I knew my end time in Hunter had begun.

From the River
to the Sea

I was burning.
The cold February wind swept smuts and sparks from my bonfire on the shingle, swirling them high in the air to float downstream in the draft. I was burning what I could not sell and what it made no sense to keep.

Old magazines, a writer's jetsam; junk mail; catalogues of absurdities. Words of elegance, words of intensity, words appealing to the god of appetite. Sometimes it's hard to tell where one stops and another begins; impossible, once they all got burning on the wide, exposed creekbed at the bottom of the canyon, fir trees towering overhead, disappearing into the fog.

Sometimes I find more holiness in the secular rags, more hunger for absurdity in the religious. Never mind: they were all blackening fragments, now, burning to humus, waiting for the rains to wash the rocks.

I started throwing other things on this pile of potential humility: old manuscripts; letters written, unmailed; notes to myself, long out of date. There was a lot I should have burned that I couldn't get my hands on: letters written and mailed; sins committed; combustibles in the heart, unexpressed, sullying its flame.

I was leaving Hunter. I had a destination and a few promises. I had a good reason to be going, but, at bottom, I really didn't know why I was leaving, only that the time had come.

The damp wind shifted, blowing smoke in my face. I stirred the fire, knowing I would reek when it was over.

I thought of Raven the first time she saw a fire. It was hard to keep her from the flames. She'd chase embers in midair, catching them in her beak. They'd turned to ash by the time she caught them, so she didn't get burned enough to learn that fire is dangerous. I feared that she would dive into the fire's heart to become an incandescent explosion of ignited feathers. Perhaps she thought she was a phoenix.

If she were in her aviary now, she'd be talking to me. But she was nearly a thousand miles away in another enclosure, waiting to be released. Tom, the warden of the wilderness area, had written that she was doing well, that she liked Carol, his wife, the two little children, and his elderly golden retrievers.

But she wouldn't go near him. I knew how hard this was for Tom. He was good with birds—he had raised a blind great horned owl—which was why I placed her with him. That, and the abundant food supply in the valley, and the milder climate.

Considering how she felt about him, Tom was hesitant to release Raven. He wondered if I would come down. He didn't want to take responsibility if she went wild.

I really didn't understand this, since the whole point was to hack her back to the wild. While this is often hard to do, we were pretty sure she would make it, not only because she had been freely hunting in the woods at Hunter, but also because another raven showed up the day she arrived and was still hanging around. He sat in the big live oak tree outside the old chicken house where Raven was penned, and talked with her.

I flipped over a copy of *Publishers Weekly* so it would burn better, and wiped my nose on my sleeve.

Transporting Raven had been an adventure all its own. Muskrat and I blinded her with a flashlight in the small hours of one morning when she was perched in her aviary and deeply asleep. I had on thick leather gloves to blunt her frightened counterattack when I grabbed her. When she discovered it was me and not the monsters ravens dream of, she calmed down.

I put the affronted bird in the carrier the airline had supplied. Then we set to dismantling her freestanding perch and nest box, and packed them with her toys.

The skycap at the airport was skeptical.

"This is luggage?"

I could tell he was getting ready to give me a hard time.

I drew myself up to my full height and contrived to look down at the man, who was at least a foot taller.

"I had to buy a ticket for my bird, and this is her luggage."

The skycap chuckled, "Yes, *Ma'am*. Well, in that case . . ." He reached for the four-foot long perch.

I turned to wave at Muskrat in the Yellow Peril, and, holding Raven in her carrier, went into the airport.

Her only panicky moment was just after takeoff. Even though her wings weren't spread, she knew she was flying. But after she got used to the effortless ride, she settled down.

I had forgotten how altitude dehydrates. When we arrived at our destination, she started to complain. Her voice was so hoarse she could hardly croak. She could maneuver part of her beak between the wire openings, so I took her over to a water fountain and, as if she'd done it every day of her life, she poked out and drank.

"Erk, erk," she commented, satisfied.

She was so quiet in the car that my father asked me if she was all right.

"Are you all right, Raven?" I inquired.

"Erk," she replied.

At Tom's we set up her paraphernalia in the disused chicken house, which was really an old slope-roofed shed with a wire front. I turned her loose.

She flapped around for a bit and came to rest on my shoulder, looking at Tom with immense distrust. He was the only man besides Eric she'd seen up close, and she wasn't too sure she liked him.

He slowly reached out his hand with a bit of food, but she retreated down my back as I leaned forward to compensate.

"Bee-dee, bee-dee, *bee-dee,* BEE-DEE, BEE-DEE, *bee-dee,*" she complained in her baby-bird voice.

I had never heard this particular sentence before, but the meaning was clear: she was bewildered, apprehensive, and she certainly didn't cotton to this khaki-clad stranger. I said a quick good-bye, and fled.

Now I was about to go south again to turn her loose. . . .

Something crackled and boiled in the smoldering pile of paper and ink; ash rose from a blue flame, whirling skyward.

Ash Wednesday would come soon, and I was grateful for it. A priest friend and I would make ashes of the palms from several years. I'd burn in that small fire all the things I couldn't get my hands on to burn in this one. He'd sign me with them, repeating the ancient words of dust and more ashes that I must become before I burn clean.

I was making ashes of my life because the more light is made manifest, the more the way becomes unknown; the more unknown, the truer the knowledge given. Oh, it wasn't anti-intellectual, this burning of old print and plunging into darkness. I was on my way to a university city on the other side of the world to a new way of following down through the humus of my life the roots of what I blindly pursue. Or what pursues me.

The fire died; the dank wind blew harder from the southeast. Soon Muskrat would come. We would go inside the cabin to sit beside the wood stove. The dogs would be snoring in its warmth on the rice-straw matting; we'd have some coffee and, in the silence, we'd probably recall our trip to the coast the day before.

The mothering sea was silken gray under a silvery pall of cloud, and combers rolled in with a power that belied its calm surface. The river flowed to meet it, clear for once, its mouth making a wide breach in the sandy barrier. The broad, powerful stream of fresh water slipped under the waves with no sign of the maelstrom where the two waters mingled.

He shall defend the needy among the people; he shall rescue the poor and crush the oppressor. . . .

"Sure gonna miss you," Muskrat said, breaking the silence.

"Me too."

"Know who's gonna take your place?"

"They don't have anyone yet. Shirley said she'd stay until they do, or until they start logging."

"Never mind; we'll manage. But it isn't going to be any better where you're goin'."

I had no reply.

"Politics aside," she went on, "I understand why you *have* to leave. For your sake, and for mine."

It was this I had been dreading to speak about. As usual, she voiced what was in my mind.

"Here," I said, pulling a small package from my pocket, "this is for you."

In the jeweler's box was a gold-washed rose. There was a smaller one for me—a promotional bonus, the jeweler had said.

He shall come down like rain upon the mown field, like showers that water the earth.

The last wisps of memory dissolved as the fog condensed into mist. I heard her car engine straining on the hill. We would take Pomo and Kelly to Eric and Jane's. At the last moment they had given us reprieve, agreeing to give both dogs a home. They'd heard that I couldn't find a place for them together, and was going to have to put them down.

In his time shall the righteous flourish; there shall be abundance of peace till the moon shall be no more.

I stirred the ashes one last time and picked up my bucket to bring water from the creek. They hissed a little as I poured, absolving them of their heat. Bubbles rose through the dark mass. I turned away across the rough creekbed, climbed up the bank, and threaded my way through the dead garden in the clearing to the last of my packing.

He shall rule from sea to sea, and from the river to the ends of the earth.

I was driving to my parents' along the valley road through citrus and avocado groves. The sun was just coming over the mountains; the morning was fresh and smelled of orange blossoms.

On the telephone wires to the left, ahead of me, perched two ravens.

One was ringed; its right wing drooped slightly. I slowed the car, pulled over to the shoulder, and stopped. I got out as quietly as I could.

"Raven."

She looked at me.

It was Raven, and her mate felt her uncertainty. With appropriate arrogance, he leaned over and with his great beak, briefly touched hers. He flew.

She called, whether to me or to him I do not know, but the note was poignant. He replied, she called again. Then she flew after him across the orchards, toward the mountains and the sea.

"Good-bye, Raven," I cried, and she replied, calling as she followed the summons of her life's partner, calling until she was out of sight, and out of hearing.